DYNAMITE DOUBLES

Play **Winning Tennis** Today!

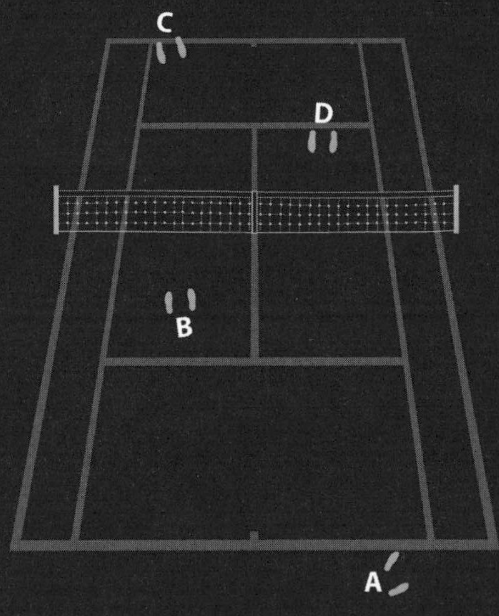

dyna

mite DOUBLES

Play Winning Tennis Today!

Dear Martha –
Be the terminator as
much as possible –
hit in front of yourself
Helle
meadowood
– 2015

By Helle Sparre

with Jim Schock

REGENT PRESS
Oakland, CA

This quotation was posted above the door to the indoor courts at KB (*Kjøbenhavns Boldklub*) where I played much of my tennis growing up:

"*tab og vind med samme sind*"

If you can meet with Triumph and Disaster
And treat those two impostors just the same
— Rudyard Kipling

"If you want to know your past, look at your present condition;
if you want to know your future, look at your present actions."
— The Buddha

DEDICATION

To

Karin, *my wife and best friend, whose love, support and encouragement allowed me this third edition of Dynamite Doubles.*

Annika, *my fabulous, fun-loving, kind daughter, who has blessed us with the 2 most adorable grandchildren, Annika Graciela and Adrian Rodolfo.*

Mor og Far (Mom and Dad), *whose continued support and love never stop. By far the best parents a child could wish for.*

With love and thanks to hundreds of my students who asked all the wonderful questions over the years that resulted in this book.

A New Book From:
DYNAMITE DOUBLES
Hellecool@comcast.net
www.dynamitedoubles.com

Dynamite Doubles: Play Winning Tennis Today!
First Edition 2004
Second Editon 2008
Third Edition 2012

ISBN 10: 1-58790-066-1
ISBN 13: 978-1-58790-066-2
LIBRARY OF CONGRESS CONTROL NUMBER: 2004100221

e-book
ISBN 10: 1-58790-191-9
ISBN 13: 978-1-58790-191-1

Dynamite Doubles: Play Winning Tennis Today! by Helle
Illustrations by Sara Kurkov
Book design by Francisco de Oliveira Mattos

Manufactured in the U.S.A.
Regent Press
2747 Regent Street
Berkeley, CA 94705
www.regentpress.net

DYNAMITE DOUBLES

contents

ROSIE CASALS is a 1966 graduate of George Washington High School in San Francisco. She established the first women's tennis team in 1965 and rose to fame in the '60s and '70s. In 1964 she entered the U.S. Women's Top Five for the first time and remained there for 11 consecutive years. In 1970, Rosie was the first-ever winner of the Virginia Slims Tournament. Three years later she became the first winner of the Family Circle Cup, receiving $30,000 the highest purse ever awarded to a female athlete. Ms. Casals resides in California, where she is President of her company, SPORTSWOMAN. She still plays in invitational tennis events.

"...one of the best"

Foreword by Rosie Casals

It's no secret that my passion for doubles was developed early in my life when, at the age of nine, I first started playing tennis on the public courts of San Francisco's Golden Gate Park. Youngsters were not allowed to play alone on a court, therefore we always had to play doubles with an adult. It actually turned out to be a great education for my tennis because it helped me develop an all-court game that served me well in both singles and doubles. Learning team-work, angles, and good shot selection eventually gave me the opportunity to play professional tennis and win twelve Grand Slam Doubles titles.

I have always loved the fast pace of serve and volley, lobs and overheads, action and reaction. I don't think anything brought me more satisfaction than executing a well-placed lob that would open up the court and allow my partner and me to take control. That's what doubles is: positioning and taking control of the court and the point.

I have known Helle for over 30 years, having first played against her on the Virginia Slims Tour in the '70s. I was always impressed with her tennis ability and her doubles skills. She had a sense for doubles, with quick hand-eye coordination, that made her one of the best. Helle Viragh has written an exciting and easy to understand doubles book that can improve anyone's game—regardless of their level. In the following pages of this exceptional book you will enjoy learning about strategy, angles, shot selection and court positioning.

I would like to congratulate Helle for writing one of the most informative and colorful doubles books and I look forward to her next session of Dynamite Doubles.

VIC SEIXAS was born in Philadelphia in 1923, and began playing tennis when he was five. A junior player of great promise, he won the Wimbledon Singles title in 1953. The following year he stunned the U.S. Open by winning all three, Singles, Doubles and Mixed Doubles. He was a member of the U.S. Avis Cup team from 1951-1957, and in 1954 led the win over the fearless Aussies. Vic teamed with Doris Hart in mixed doubles for five years during which they lost only one match while winning three Wimbledon titles and three U.S. titles. Vic teamed with Tony Trabert to win the Australian, the U.S. and the French Open. Asked about his doubles success, he replied, "First get a good partner. Second, tell your partner, 'if you can reach it—take it.'"

"...impressed by her teaching ability"

Foreword by Vic Seixas

Just when you think you know it all, along comes someone who increases your knowledge. So it is with *Dynamite Doubles,* a well written book by Helle, designed to improve one's doubles play by teaching a system that's easy to understand and makes good sense.

I've known Helle since coming to California in 1989. She has always impressed me as a player. Now, I am more impressed by her teaching ability and understanding of doubles strategy.

One thing that prevailed throughout the book was her good sense of humor, that alone makes reading it a pleasure. She obviously enjoys teaching tennis and I am sure this comes through to her students.

I always thought the most important factor in winning doubles was to get a good partner! With Helle's system, those who play it can team up together and have success right away. Her "zones" are a different approach to doubles strategy and allow partners to adjust to each other almost immediately. Throughout the book, she stresses "patience" and "percentage," two vital elements of successful doubles. I particularly like the idea of the "terminator" and "workhorse" which clearly defines the role of each partner.

In summary I would urge any tennis player who wants to see immediate improvement in his or her doubles play to read *Dynamite Doubles.*

Vic

Helle at Wimbledon. You'll understand her sense of humor when you learn the "trophy" she's holding is a coffee urn from the NBC Television Facility in the background.

who the heck is Helle?

Helle (it's pronounced HELL-uh) tells her story better than anyone else can and I want to introduce you to the woman who's going to help you improve your doubles tennis game by this afternoon. Unlike many tennis pros who enjoyed success on the tour, she's been able to translate her skills to hundreds and hundreds of students who have improved their game and their appreciation of the sport of tennis.

Helle began playing tennis at the age of six in her native Denmark, and by age nineteen she was the Number One ranked player in her country. The following year she retained that ranking and was playing professional tennis all over the world, advancing to the round of 32 at Wimbledon. How does a young girl get involved with tennis and what keeps her going? Here's her story:

Just after I turned six, my Dad shortened the handle of an old Dunlop Maxply wooden racquet. I carried that racquet with me everywhere I went and used an old grey (formerly white) fuzzless tennis ball. My parents belonged to the oldest club in Denmark, Copenhagen's Ballclub, Kjøbenhavns Boldklub, founded in 1876 and I hit against the "wall" while they were out playing.

"Torben Ulrich, the Number One player in Denmark at the time, used to come by and practice at the same wall. I admired him a lot because his tennis was not only speed and strength, it included grace and beauty as well.

Torben Ulrich

"Many years later Torben made a video about 'The Wall' and how to practice against it or with it. I consider myself extremely fortunate to have started my tennis at the wall and to have met this wonderful man. Since that time in Copenhagen, I have spent many memorable moments with this tennis master. He has been an inspiration to me all my life and I am forever grateful for all he has taught me.

"I met my first tennis partner at the wall when I was nine years old. Her name was Sys and her father had called KB and asked if there was anyone about his daughter's age she could play with. The people at KB had seen me at the wall many times and suggested that we meet each other. So we did.

"We started hitting together against the wall and became regular partners. However, it was many weeks later before it occurred to us that we could actually go out on a real tennis court! It just came to us that we did not have to stay at the wall because now there were two of us and that's all it takes to play tennis! We took the grey ball and strolled out on a tennis court and that's how it all began. Since we had only one ball, we soon learned to keep it in play, rather than spend all our time chasing it and picking it up.

"Sys and I became best friends and we dominated the Junior Tennis world in Denmark for the next eight years. We also managed to irk a lot of managers and workers at the various clubs around the country who did not appreciate our 'great sense of humor.'

"However, tennis gave me a way of life and I am grateful for that and for the many varied and exciting experiences throughout my tennis career. I traveled all over the world, I met many wonderful people who have influenced me and I am still in love with the game today. At 47 I am still excited about and still learning the game of tennis.

FOTO H. PETERSEN

"Whether you're a parent or not, I must tell you that my parents helped me so much by supporting my interest in the sport in a very non-pressure way and for that I will always be extremely grateful. I was able to make a lot of decisions during my tennis career (not all of them great) and perhaps the biggest one of all was when, at age seventeen, I decided to stay in the United States after a tournament, and not return to Denmark to finish school. As a mother, I can really understand how much trust, understanding and courage it took for my mother and father to put aside their anxiety and worry and let me do it my way. Through the years, many of them stormy and unsure, they were always there for me.

Sys is on the left.

"I married Botond Viragh, a polished and worldly Hungarian, when I was nineteen. We were married for 30 years and behind us are tough times and good times—all of them learning experiences which have ultimately benefitted us greatly. We are blessed with a wonderful daughter.

Annika now has two children of her own, Annika Graciela and Adrian Rodolfo. These two grandchildren of mine fill my heart with joy and laughter and make time stand still. Being a mormor (grandma) is the best thing in the world.

Annika played tennis as a junior and is is now teaching tennis with me at the same club. How cool is that! And our latest student and future tennis star is little Annika!

•••

After Annika was born, Helle decided it was time to stay home a while, concentrate on family life and maybe "teach a little tennis." Twenty-some years later, she's still "teaching a little tennis"—actually, a *lot* of tennis, and having a great time. She'll tell you she's *learning* a lot of tennis, too, explaining that teaching has helped her understand the game more than playing on the tour. "If I knew then what I know now...wow*!*" is how she puts it.

Teaching has made her study the game more than she ever did before. When she was a touring pro, playing with professionals, she acted and reacted instinctively, creatively, without much thought, discussion or analysis. Since she began teaching, she's made some great discoveries—things all tennis players should know, but haven't been told. Helle has some wonder-

ful *new* ideas about the game of doubles and after developing her system over a ten year period wants now to share them with a larger audience. She has a lot of enthusiasm and a guarantee:

> "I promise you will improve your doubles game immediately. You will expand your understanding and knowledge of the game, and you will have a lot more fun playing and winning."

The idea for this book was born on a sparkling afternoon on the teaching court at the Scott Valley Swimming and Tennis Club in Mill Valley, California, a few minutes north of the Golden Gate Bridge.

Helle was teaching a doubles strategy lesson and listening to the same basic questions that always come up:

1. what should I have done?
2. where should I have been?
3. how could I have gotten that?
4. whose was that?

This time when the students began asking questions, she realized there was a pattern to her answers and that with minor systematic changes, her students could improve their game and understanding of it immediately. She realized, in that flash that she was *instinctively* moving and repositioning herself during the point more than the students, regardless of who was hitting the ball. She stopped right there and went back, point-by-point, shot-by-shot, stroke-by-stroke, analyzing the type of steps and moves she was making in order to anticipate the next shot.

Her students immediately saw that she was moving a great deal more than they were *after she had hit the ball and while the ball was in the air.* She was less stressed and in much better position when it came time to react and anticipate her opponents' shot. The result: more time to prepare for her next shot. She also moved when the ball was *not* coming to her, when her *partner* was going to hit the ball. She used that time to get in position before her opponents could hit their next shot.

This is the key to her system: Be ready and balanced at the right place before the opponents' next shot.

She *especially* noticed her students moved a great deal less when the ball was in the air—whether it was coming toward them or away from them and they became panicky, surprised and rushed when it was time to hit the ball. They made the shots sometimes, but had no plan

above: Helle at age 10, Kjöbenhavns Boldklub.
below: Helle, Bornholm Open, 1975.

as to placement or strategy. That meant they weren't balanced when hitting the ball—which made it difficult to execute the shot.

Beginning that day, she continued to analyze her own moves, footwork patterns and mental processes while playing a point. She began to chart these moves on a piece of paper, then *lots* of paper. She didn't do this for a day or a week or a month, but for years and from it she has developed a system of playing doubles you've never heard before.

She calls it her "Dynamite Doubles System" and if you and your partner follow it, you'll take your game to another level and discover the true meaning of teamwork. It's designed to make you focus on where to be for the next shot, dividing court responsibility between you and your partner, as well as placement of your shot. In other words, concentrate on playing the odds, rather than on winning or losing the point. Here's her promise, stick to the system and winning doubles will follow. You'll stop blaming yourself or your partner as the two of you become one and play each point as a team. Think of it, you'll be at the right place at the right time. You'll know what shot to look for and you'll challenge your opponents to hit the most difficult shot every single time. Result:

You win*!*

YOU'LL ACTUALLY

BE ABLE TO BEAT

BETTER TENNIS PLAYERS*!*

We all know there are certain partners we like to play with because we feel we "click" with them. With Helle's system, you'll understand doubles better and be able to "click" with most partners and make the very best of the situation. You'll play more tennis, enjoy it more and your skills will increase.

Helle has written this book for everyone—men and women of all levels of play and all ages who want to play tennis lifelong, and for coaches and teachers who would like to have a system for teaching winning doubles.

After all, if you know the Where–What–Where Rule...

WHERE TO BE
positioning: up and back

WHAT TO COVER
court coverage responsibility

WHERE TO HIT
short selection and placement

you'll have great command of your game. The other thing is that you'll stop asking those awful questions (was that mine, etc. etc.) and begin to ask yourself THE TWO MOST IMPORTANT QUESTIONS IN DOUBLES, "Where is the ball?" and "Where should I be?"

The answers are in this book. From now on you'll always know *where* to be in relation to the oncoming ball, *what* part of the court is yours to cover and *where* to hit it.

Helle's system is based on achieving the best court coverage possible at any given time, rather than on who has the strong or weak forehand or backhand. In a way, it's a lot like two-person volleyball, where the two of you are constantly setting the ball up for one another and defending when the ball is in the opponents' court.

Dynamite Doubles fosters a team spirit between you and your partner, and this book opens up doubles tennis as a far more intriguing game than you ever dreamed. You will be in the right place, taking only balls that are yours, and hitting them to the right place. Even if you don't *hit* the ball to the right place, you will learn how to deal with it by *being* in the right place, ready to defend against any shot from your opponents.

By the way, the title for this book has a story, too. As you know, the national flag of Denmark is a white cross on a red field. The Danish national cheering song (you didn't know?) contains these lines:

(We are red, we are white
We are Danish dynamite!)

It was not a large leap from there.

Good luck to all of you. If you'd like, write or Email Helle (dynamitedoubles@yahoo.com or www.dynamitedoubles.com) to let her know how you're doing. You'll get a reply. That's the kind of person she is.

Jim Schock
January, 2004
Mill Valley, California

JIM SCHOCK is a former news executive and producer for ABC-TV Sports. He had not played tennis since college, "...but when I was readying my first tennis broadcast, I was impressed by how the speed and power of the game was tempered by grace and elegance. Some points were pure poetry." When he was introduced to Helle and her system, "I had a sense Dynamite Doubles could instantly make the doubles game easier to play, more exciting, less confusing and a better experience for average players." He immediately agreed to help transfer Helle's unique skills from the court to the printed page. Mr. Schock is also a novelist and screenwriter, and resides in Mill Valley, California.

Jim Schock in his tennis-playing days. Mr. Schock no longer smokes, but admits he has become addicted to watching Helle's students consistently win lots of doubles matches.

definitions

Here are some definitions of terms I use in this book. You probably know them, but in case you don't, familiarize yourself with them because you'll be seeing a lot more of them before we finish.

the ready position

Balance yourself, relax, be alert. Stand with your feet comfortably apart. The space between the inside of your feet at shoulder width. Keep your weight on the balls of your feet, bending your knees slightly inward. Keep your racquet in front of you, pointed straight and keep both hands on it. Relax your grip. Your shoulders should be aligned over your knees. Keep your head steady and your eyes focused on the ball. You can move in any direction from the ready position.

the middle T

The middle T is the point where the service line and the center service line meet. This is a vital target and you need to know how and when to aim for it.

the workhorse

The player diagonally across from the ball. This is new terminology. With my system, you'll always know what your role is and knowing that, you will know where to play on the court. A lot more on this in a bit.

the terminator

The player straight across from the ball. Another new term, and it doesn't sound like it belongs on a tennis court, does it? Well, get used to it because knowing when you are one will help you win points.

Helle ready at the net with partner Andrea Barnes serving. PHOTO BY BRENDA LAROSE

the split step

This is the ready position In Action. It's that little hop you do in hopscotch. It is a timing step you execute in order to put your body in the ready position. During a point, it enables you to get ready to move in any direction to any ball. *How to use:* You split-step facing the ball and the person who is about to hit the ball. *When to use:* You split-step every time an opponent it about to hit the ball, even on serve. Watch your opponent's racquet, and just as it is about to come forward to strike the ball, you make a little hop. As you land, turn and move to the oncoming ball.

Practice pausing/slowing down every time the ball bounces in your opponents' court. Then you are ready to time the important split-step/hop to your opponent's racquet swing.

You can always split-step again if you have the time.

Important: Never remain planted in your split-step. You need to turn and move as you come down from your hop. Split-step, then turn your shoulders and move toward the oncoming ball.

The split-step is a vital part of the rhythm and timing of the point. After you hit a shot, you need to recover and balance yourself before the next ball comes. Your sideways recovery steps function as several split-steps put together. The split-step sets up the entire footwork in preparation for any shot. You can get a sense of the rhythm ...split, turn, move, hit. Split, split, split, turn, move, hit. split, split, turn and so on.

When you watch a pro match on TV, notice how the service returner always makes that little hop as the server strikes the ball. The pros do it all through their matches. After each shot as they recover, they shuffle back—which is lots of little split steps—and then slow down to one timed split-step/hop just as the opponent's racquet comes forward to strike the ball. Watch Serena and Andre for example.

I am emphasizing the split-step because it is a crucial point for good preparation, good footwork and good execution. If you are not using the sideways recovery steps in your game now, start doing so immediately. You'll find it easier to split-step at the right moment. In a serve and volley situation, a server sprints forward approximately three-four steps, slows down, pauses as the ball bounces, and makes a split-step (hop) as her opponent's racquet swings forward at the ball. Now the server is ready to turn and move diagonally forward for the return of serve to hit either a volley or half-volley.

I like to think of the split-step as a moment where I can let go of my last shot and focus totally on reading what is happening in front of me and react quickly and appropriately.

1

LESSON ONE

a great day for tennis

hi. *Good morning. Beautiful day for tennis, isn't it? That a new racquet? How's the grip? How does it feel to hit with it? Good. Show me how you hold it. Forehand. Good. Let me see your backhand grip. Been playing long? You play mostly singles or doubles? Doubles? Great! How's your serve? Mmm. What do you think your strengths are on the court? I see. What do you think your weaknesses might be? Let me ask you, do you like to play tennis? Why do you play? How often do you play?*

Okay, enough.

When I meet a new student for the first time, before we start stretching or hitting balls, I like to find out a little bit about them—you, in this case. Tennis players come in every size and shape imaginable. Each of you has a "court personality" and you have strengths and weaknesses in your game. Everybody has strengths and weaknesses, even the pros. On any level of play, the object is always to maximize your strengths, minimize your weaknesses.

If we were meeting on the court for the first time, I'd try to find out how you see yourself as a player, and learn something about your attitude toward the game. I'd try to find out if you enjoy playing. Sadly, lots of tennis players consider playing a drag, but make themselves play because their perception is that tennis is a glamourous form of exercise. Listen to me: Tennis is a lot more than that.

While we're talking, I may check your grip, study how comfortable you are in a tennis atmosphere. I also "read your shoes." You would be surprised how much your shoes can reveal about your game. If you have an old gray pair, it usually means you use them for things other than tennis and might not be all that serious about your game.

Still "reading" shoes, if I see worn-out toes, it means you play a lot, but you don't keep your equipment up to par. If you're wearing brand-new shoes, you're either a brand-new student who wants to look good, or it may be you're experienced and knew it was time for new footwear. I'm going to ask.

The reason I do all this, get to know as much about you as I can, is because your personality and sense of the game greatly affects how well you play and how good you can become. The challenge in teaching people to play tennis is the challenge of helping individuals one at a time, making them better. In order to do that, we should get to know each other a little. That's why the front pages tell you something about me. In case you skipped them, at some point you should go back and read them in order to check out who is giving you all this advice.

My teaching is not an assembly-line. I *never* give orders to "do-this, do-that, practice-this, practice-that, see you next time." As my students will tell you, no two of my lessons are exactly the same because I always try to fit the instruction to the individual need of each student. There are two great benefits to that. First, the student benefits from individual instruction. Two, the teacher/pro never gets bored. These are pretty good rewards.

Anyway, after we meet and chat a bit and I have some idea what your game is about, the next thing I do is introduce you to the tennis court. As simple as that sounds, it is actually a complete re-orientation—a brand new way to look at the old court. After I explain this, your tennis game begins to improve and neither you, nor your game, will ever be the same.

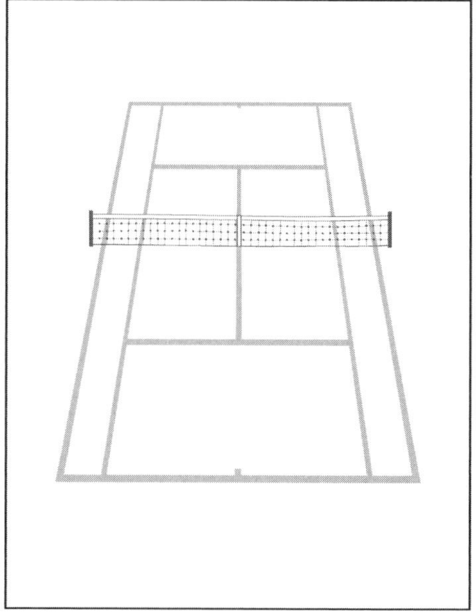

court geography.

Here's your new tennis court. What's that? It looks just like the same one you've been playing on. It is, but let me suggest you look at it in a different way because there's a good chance you have not *really* oriented yourself to the full playing area. Here's a clue: Explore the possibilities which lie beyond the painted lines.

REMEMBER: THE LINES ARE ONLY FOR THE BALLS! There is a great deal of playing area beyond the lines. The third dimension of the game—*Altitude*—involves the height of the ball, be it a zinger that skims the net, or a sky-high lob.

The area where you play looks like this:

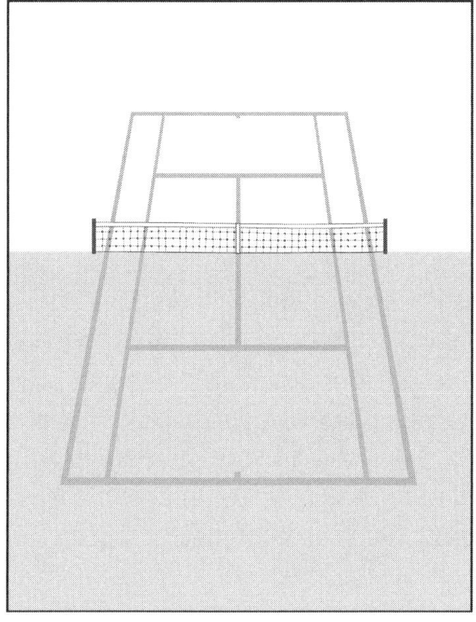

"outside the lines".

The shaded portion indicates your playing area. As you can see, it's a lot more than just the lines, isn't it? This is actually the first clue about Dynamite Doubles. It's the new Landscape of the Court. How well you perform on this landscape, especially in the shaded areas, can largely determine the outcome of your future doubles tennis games. Patrolling the right area, being in the right place at the right time *is more important than anything else.*

While we're talking turf here, let me just advise you to learn how to scope out the courts on which you play. A narrow space between the court and the side tells me to watch out for sharp angles, since I won't be able to run them down. Similarly, the space behind the baseline can dictate how you play. If there is little space (less than 21 feet), you must be quicker and you will have to take deep balls on the rise. If there is plenty of room, you have more time to run down lobs and get to balls before the second bounce. The same goes for your opponent, of course, so you may be able to use the limitation of the court dimensions to your advantage. Turn a negative into a positive.

what this book is *not* about.

I won't be talking about strokes in this book. You know how to hit the ball. Your local pro has taught you the basics.

I *will* be teaching you what to do with what you've learned so far, but we won't discuss how to stroke a tennis ball. In fact, right here and now I'm advising you to not even *think* about "strokes" per se. I will be talking about *moving.* Tennis is not just smacking the ball. I am going to insist you think about moving to the right place on the court at the right time, and aiming at the correct target each time you hit the ball. I will show you how to do this and when you do it, your strokes will be better, I promise you.

Let's go back to the turf. The shaded areas represent more than the playing areas. They represent specific strategies, depending on Location, and Location is the key because there are only three things you can do on the court. You can:

ATTACK.

DEFEND.

BE NEUTRAL (SET-UP).

That's easy. Why doesn't someone actually lay out the tennis court so players can understand where and when they need to be Attacking, Defending or Setting-Up? Well, someone has. And here it is:

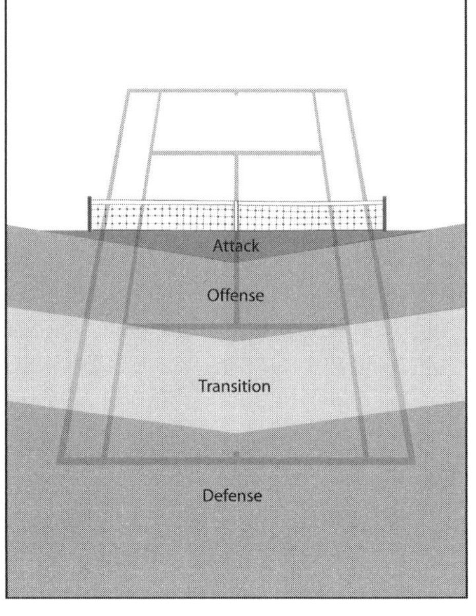

I'll explain these zones in greater depth in a bit, but for now, look at the overview. The day you and your partner recognize these zones, and begin playing Dynamite Doubles, is the day you begin to improve your game far beyond anything you've known. You won't have to hit the ball any harder, or run farther. You'll never bump into anyone on the court ever again.

Let's add one more element to our court geography:

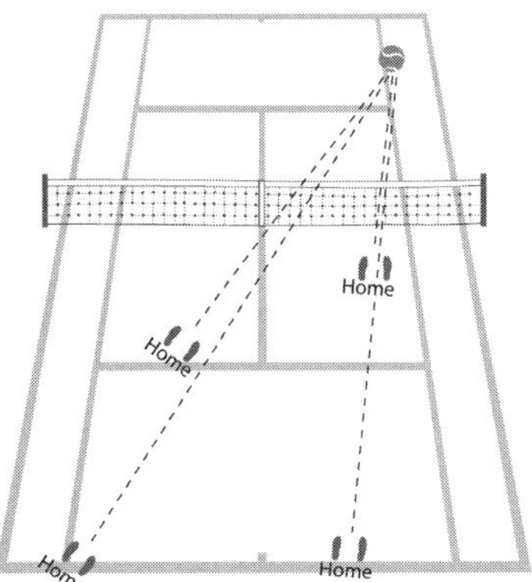

See those little feet with "home" written behind them? Those are your "homes" where you hang out on the court. You're always safe at home. You have two homes and your partner has two.

Depending on where the ball is in your opponents' court, you and your partner need to be in one of your homes. If you are in one of your homes before your opponent strikes the ball, you have a good chance to get to any ball she hits.

Those are the basics. There's nothing difficult to understand and very little to remember. If you know these homes and zones, and go out on the court and put them into your game, you'll be winning more doubles than ever before.

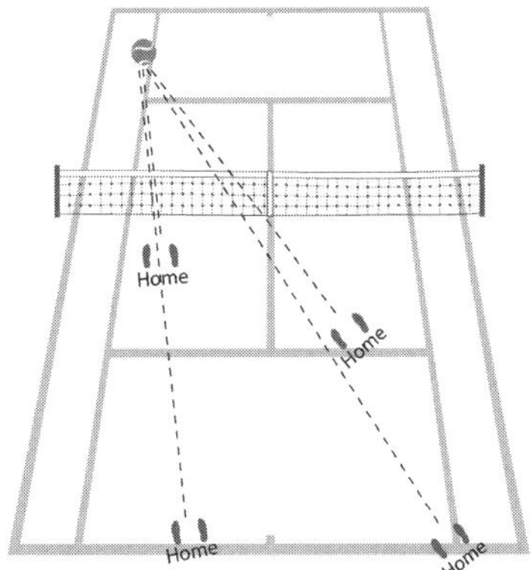

However, you might want to know something more about what they do and why they work, and how they can do everything I say they can. Well, now that we know each other a little better, *and* you've looked at the tennis court in a new, interesting way, let's go on to Lesson Two.

HELLE'S HINTS

At the end of each chapter, I'll be giving you some tips on what to practice to help develop the strategies I'll be discussing. I want to say it now and I'll be reminding you often, that this is a series of steps you can take to increase your strategic skills. This goes for both you and your partner(s). There's nothing complicated here, but there is an order of march that I've found works with my students. I want you to have the benefit of those fifteen years I've been shouting and moving people around the court.

The other thing is that if you have a problem or find a way to add a nice touch here and there to the Dynamite Doubles System, I hope you'll drop me a line. The address to write to is in the front of the book.

2

LESSON TWO

tennis: love it or leave it

Remember, this book is going to eliminate those four basic questions that plague doubles tennis players:

1. what should I have done?
2. where should I have been?
3. how could I have gotten that?
4. whose was that?

First, let's take another look at the Game itself. There are two remarkable facts about tennis. The first is there are no owners, no legion of cigar-puffing men in suits who manipulate players under contract to them. There is no block of a few business people creating the rules, making or breaking careers. The game is freer, truly a test of skill between individuals.

The other remarkable thing is that nearly everybody who plays the game is a loser. There is only *one* winner each time out. One. In the case of doubles, one team of two people. *Everybody else in the tournament has lost along the way.* So that means one person (or one team) is happy, everybody else goes home defeated and discouraged.

Well, it doesn't work *exactly* that way.

So why do we still come back? It's pretty simple to me and I hope I can make it easier for you. We don't have to win the entire tournament to feel like a winner. If you had to, it would be difficult to field enough players for a tournament. The thrill is to give it your best and grow as a tennis player each time out. You are challenging yourself.

With this concept (maybe it's just an attitude adjustment) you can be a winner in my book every time you step on the court.

Tennis can be a game of great excitement and bring a lifetime of pleasure. But tennis, like life, isn't perfect. And, like life, it can get in a rut, lose its sparkle and become a drudge. That happens when your game goes sour, most especially when your *doubles* game stops being fun and exhilarating and turns into sharp looks, bitter words, frustration and disappointment. The person who is supposed to be your partner becomes part of the problem. Nothing nor anyone goes right. In place of a pleasant and character-building hour or so of exercise and fun, it becomes an arena of hostility and gritted teeth.

Relax, it probably doesn't mean the end of the world. It probably *does* mean your game needs some attention to get it—and you—back on track. Your serve may be fine, your strokes sharp and keen, your footwork sound. So what's wrong? Most likely it's that part of your body you work the least when you play doubles—your mind, your head, the old bean, the gray matter. When you're not getting good results with your tennis game, it can mess you up, on and off the court.

Good results have to do with your performance, not with the outcome. So, the key is to set performance goals that you can achieve, that are within your reach so you can accomplish some of them each time you step onto the court. When winning or losing becomes the sole matter, you are setting yourself up for defeat. We would love to win the match, of course, but as soon as that thought has passed you, you must come back to the present and work point by point, moment by moment and achieve small task goals on your path to success.

help is on the way.

At the club where I teach we've had phenomenal success with my Dynamite Doubles Strategy and Tactics System.

Now, not all members have adopted my system, but what's really interesting is that "C" players are all of a suddenly beating "B" players. And "B" players are beating "A" players—*based solely* on using this system, not on any other improvement in their game.

I keep using the word "system" because it's a plan, a basic idea you take with you when you step onto the court. Use it and you'll always know what to look for, where to position yourself and what to do when the ball comes to you. Right now, understand that in doubles, the easiest part of the whole game is hitting the ball. We can all do that and do it well, in practice, during lessons, when there is no pressure. If not, take a lesson. *Harder than hitting the ball is the job of being in the right place at the right time, knowing what part of the court is yours to cover, and having an idea of where the best place is to hit it.*

It's right at this concept where many great singles players usually lose it in doubles. The singles player is used to seeing an open court as soon as an opponent is pulled wide to one side. In doubles, two partners cover for each other, and the openings are not so simple to find. There's a lot more to think about, a longer, less-instinctive process that goes on because you have a partner to think about. You have to be more patient and unselfish, and the court seems smaller with two players on each side. Your singles instincts will fail you here. There's more to understand about the game than one-on-one battling.

Maybe nobody told you this, but I'm sure you sensed it while you were out on the court at one time or another. When a winning point shoots between you and your partner and all you can do is exchange looks and apologize to each other. Or when you saw an opportunity to win a point appear and then disappear almost immediately and left you with the strange feeling there was *something* you should be doing at times like that. Well...you're right.

Look, there are only five simple strategies to my Dynamite Doubles. They're easy to remember:

STRATEGY 1

cover 100% of your court when the ball is in your opponents' court.

I'll show you and your partner how to do that, easily and confidently so that from the other side of the net you'll look and act like a *team,* two players moving and winning points with apparent ease, interacting to form an unbeatable combination.

STRATEGY 2

fulfill your role responsibilities.

First, you have to know what they are. Merely getting the ball back over the net doesn't qualify you as a responsible doubles player. You have to know where *and when* to move and so does your partner. I'll take care of this responsibility thing for you both.

STRATEGY 3

maneuver for high percentage shots.

Hold on to your visor...*Taking or leaving the right ball is more important than how well you execute your stroke.* REMEMBER: Getting ready for the next shot is what it's all about. Taking the wrong ball will leave you out of position and you will be vulnerable for the next shot. Learning and executing the correct strategy and tactics of doubles play will win more games than glorious, showy strokes. If you happen to be very good at that, it won't hurt your game, of course. But try to begin to understand right now that friends who don't play quite up to your level can still beat you. This book tells you how and why that's possible.

STRATEGY 4

move diagonally. turn and face your opponent who is hitting the ball, and split-step/hop as her racquet swings towards the ball.

Sometimes I call this the Belly Shot. You turn your body and face the ball so your opponent could use your belly button for a target. Ditto the Between-the-Eyes Shot. Point your racquet straight out at the ball from the Ready Position as if your racquet is a radar ball detector (see "Definitions"). Watch your opponent's racquet preparation, and be ready to make your split-step/hop as her racquet moves forward to hit the ball.

Individually, these are easy moves. We can all make them. What is a mystery to most doubles players is how to time these moves, together with our partner and in perfect timing to an opponent's hit. There are only a couple of things to understand that will solve this mystery forever. The explosive part of Dynamite Doubles comes from knowing *where* you should be, in relation to your partner, your opponents, and the ball. Be in the right place all of the time and your game improves immediately.

STRATEGY 5

"bisect the plane."

No, I don't mean cut a 747 in half, but you can cut your losses by a lot more than that if you are READY, READ (the opponent's feet and racquet), and REACT (to the ball) — three easy-to-do essentials that lead to winning points. What I'm going to tell you about these five strategies is simple. It's easy to understand and when you put them into practice, you'll turn your doubles game around *immediately*. But remember those three R's.

READY!

READ!

REACT!

HELLE'S HINTS

As a card-, chess-, and backgammon-player, I have learned to play the odds. If you don't have odds and percentages to guide you, then you're at the mercy of your instincts. In all of the above games and in the game of tennis, that spells trouble for all except the thinnest layer of players at the top. Leave your instincts for choosing a husband or playing the stock market. Trust common sense and play the percentages.

3

LESSON THREE

meet a new old friend

Don't jump in your tennis togs yet. I want to introduce you to an old friend. You may think you know this entity, the tennis court, but rather than a passing look—I want you to get to know it *intimately*. And I want to start by asking you how big a tennis court is. Really.

Okay, maybe you forgot. It's 78 feet, baseline to baseline. It is 27 feet wide for singles and 36 feet wide for doubles. The net is three feet high at the middle and six inches higher at the ends.

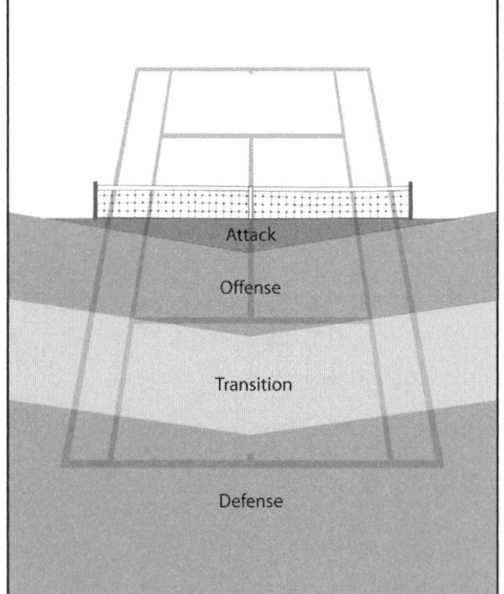

That's the size many players think it is. Actually, it "plays" a lot larger than that, but a lot of club players forget that which brings me to my first important point. *From now on I want you to begin thinking about the court in a different way.* You know where the lines are, you can even "sense" them during a game without much trouble. What you don't know is that the lines aren't as important as you may have thought they were. What's more important? **Zones.** Here's the new court you're playing on. It may look the same to your opponents, but it's much different-looking for you because now it's not just some pleasant geometry on the surface, it's a series of **zones**. These zones are your ticket to winning your next doubles game this afternoon—and a lot more wins after that. Let's take a look.

Let me show you what happens when you divide the court

into zones. You're playing your regular game and you hear that old familiar phrase, "Come to the net!" Perhaps you say it; perhaps your partner does, it doesn't matter. What matters is no one knows how far to come. Some players come to the attack zone, others stop in the transition zone and many come up side-by-side with their partner. Now it's easy to see that "Come to the net" means come to the offense zone and defend that zone at any cost. Now that's fun! Not too close to the net and not too far away. Zones work. Zones are good. Zones help you and your partner to be in the right place at the right time and isn't that what doubles is all about?

the offense zone.

Let's stay in the offense zone. Here's where you and your partner want to be and where you want to play the most tennis. This is the area where you'll build up the point. You can get to any ball your opponents hit from here and you'll be able to volley most shots. This means you will be giving opponents little time to react. You're in the driver's seat, in charge. This is the turf where you set up your winners, take charge of the game, establish control and patience.

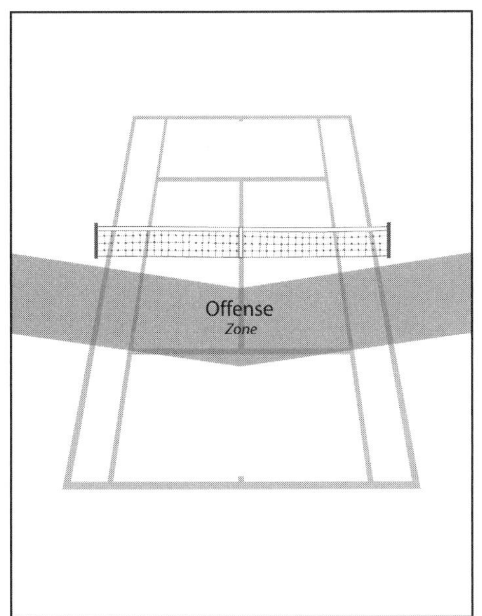

The offense zone is your most effective zone. This will become a lot more evident as we go along. For now think of it as not-too-close, not-too-far-back—just right. Later on I'll explain *exactly* where you and your partner need to be.

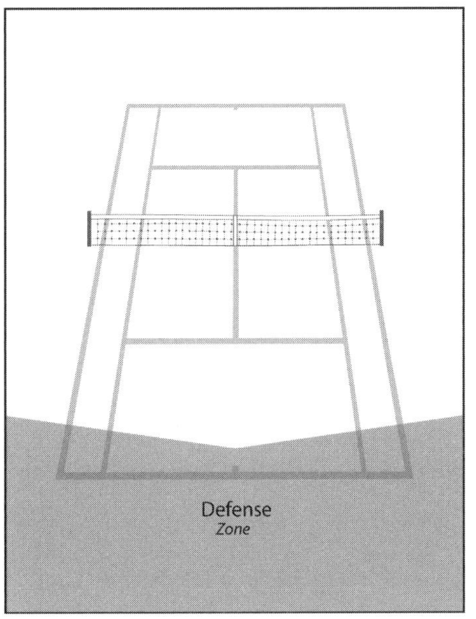

the defense zone.

Take a look at the defense zone. Notice how only a small portion of the actual court is in this zone and that the zone extends far beyond the court lines. The lines are there just to keep the ball in, but they have nothing to do with where you and your partner can play. An awful lot of winning doubles begin with one or both of you outside the boundaries. This is a major zone. Don't worry, you won't trip over the lines. (*Except* on clay courts in Europe where lines are *nailed* on the court and at times the tape is loose and you can trip. I've done it*!* You are not a true clay court player unless you have scabbed knees.)

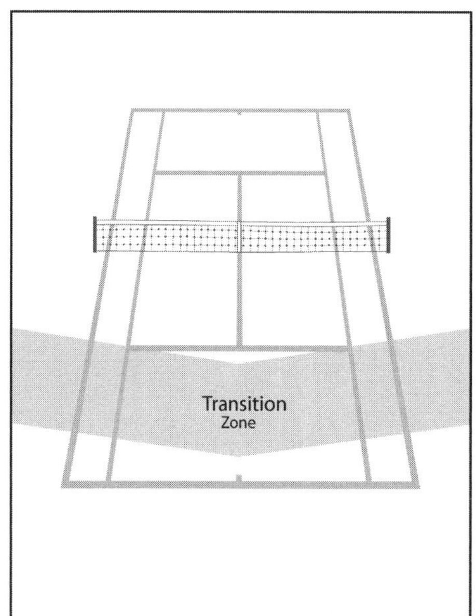

the transition zone.

As the name implies, this is a place on the court where you go through to hit a ball *and that's all*. After your stroke, you get out of there. I'll tell you more about that later, but this is where you go when you're changing zones. When you're here, think, "I'm in transition."

This is where most balls bounce so if you're standing here when opponents hit, the result will be a lot of balls coming at your feet. *You're a non-moving target.* Stand here when opponents hit and you cannot volley effectively...nor can you hit a ground stroke. However, if you move into transition from defense to hit a ball, chances are very good you'll be making an effective shot. Think of the transition zone as a place where you're transitioning from defense to offense or from offense to defense.

There are times when you move backwards from offense into transition for an overhead and return to offense after your shot. Similarly, there are times when you're in defense and must move forward to transition for a shot and return to defense.

Remember, when you're in that part of the landscape we're calling the transition zone, you'll always be en route to another zone. After you hit a ball from here, always recover to a major zone, offense or defense.

the attack zone.

Okay, I admit it, I tell my students this is also known as THE KILLER ZONE. This is where everybody wants to be. In football it's inside the opponent's 20 yard

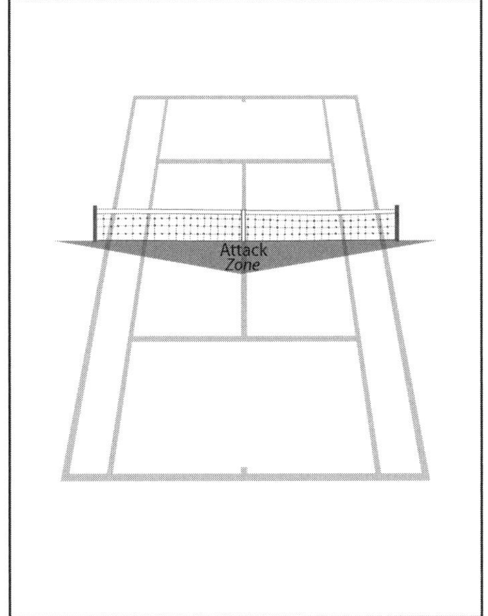

them on the court. I realize, it's something more to think about at first, but, honestly, after a short while, it'll come to you (and your partner) and they'll be like old friends and you'll swear you knew them all your tennis-playing life.

Zones are the key to your court coverage, so let's meet each one of them, as ABC SPORTS says, "Up close and personal."

line and it's called the Red Zone—and a team is supposed to put some points on the scoreboard. You have to work to earn your right to get into this zone.

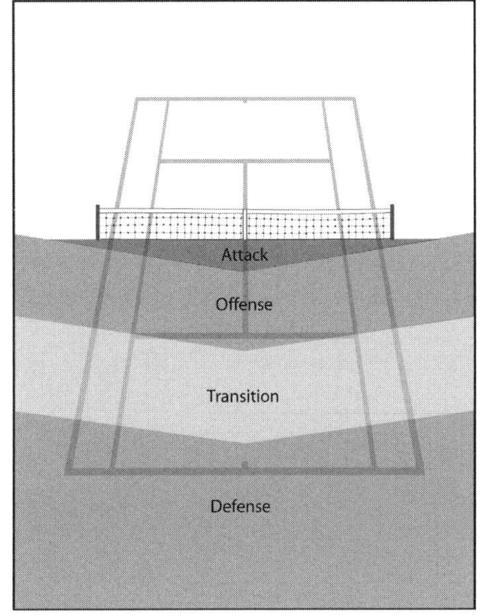

learn the zones.

Study them, look at the drawings, get to know where the zones are. Begin right now to picture

HELLE'S HINTS

When you look at the illustrations and when you first try to visualize the zones on the playing court, understand two easy facts:

First, the offense and defense zones are the major zones. During the course of your tennis-playing, you will be hitting many, many shots from these two zones.

Last, the transition and attack zones are one-shot zones, that is, one-shot and you're out of there, moving into a major zone.

Simple. Effective. Powerful knowledge.

4

LESSON FOUR

zoned for success

Look at the court coverage chart and don't panic. It's actually a road map I want you to have in your head. I want you to put it there consciously every time you practice or play from now on. In time, it will become automatic and you'll never remember when you didn't know the Secret of the Zones. (Sounds like a *Twilight Zone* episode, doesn't it?)

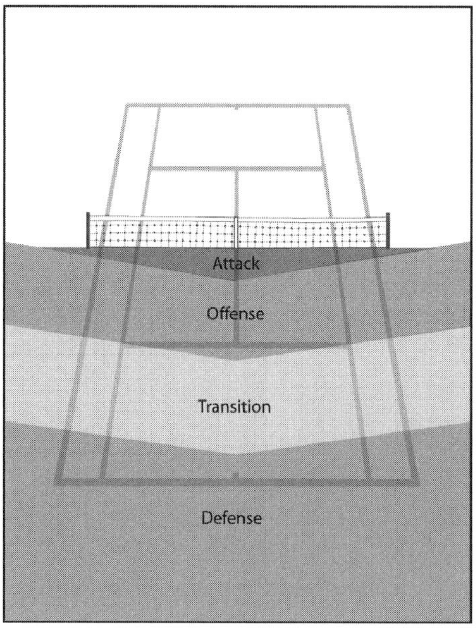

the defense zone.

The biggest area, of course, is the defense zone. It's not that much of the actual between-the-lines tennis court, but the area to the fences is what's key here. The defense zone is a major zone and you may hit more than one shot from here. If you're playing most of your doubles tennis here, you're working very hard and you're limiting yourself quite a bit. You don't hit many winners from here, *especially* if you're playing a team that knows my system. And you can have your great drive and your great lob and your great angled topspin dipper. You'll only win a point when your opponents make a mistake. And just look at the ground you have to cover. Remember what I said about the game being played *beyond* the lines? Here you get a good look at what's really involved. Your commitment is to cover everything from inside the lines of the tennis court, out to the wide open spaces that stretch all the way to the fences. Play in this zone only and you play hard and you play tired. You'll always be out there for long matches.

It is not an effective use of energy, but in certain situations, you may have to play from here in order to win. You have more time back here and a better chance of getting the ball back across the net—especially against stronger players. If you want, think of this area here as a great neutralizing zone where play can be slowed down and you can introduce that other element so important in tennis—Patience. From here you can challenge opponents' Patience, create an edge for your team.

The important thing to remember for now is that *if one of you is in trouble in the defense zone,* the other needs to be there, too. There is a lot of real estate to defend and you must defend it *together.*

One of the most frustrating things I see is when two players are involved in a strenuous game and one of them is in the defense zone and her partner is a spectator in the attack or offense zone. Get your feet and the rest of your equipment moving and get back there to help!

In truth, there is more area in the defense zone than both of you can defend and looking at the real size of this zone, you can appreciate how difficult it is to play winning doubles from these wastelands. It's bigger than all the other zones combined.

You do have more time to get to track the ball and get to it before it bounces twice, and you can slow the pace down against stronger players, but your are extremely vulnerable to any short balls and angles.

ever thought of this?

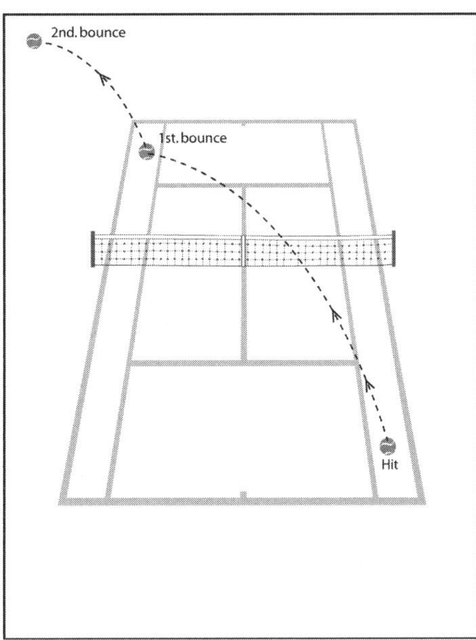

The lines on the court are boundaries *for the balls.* The fences are boundaries for the players. Players can run down balls way beyond the lines of the court. Remember, the ball is alive and playable until the second bounce. When you are in trouble, running balls down toward the second bounce gives you the maximum time to execute the best possible shot.

learn the territory.

First, if you serve and stay back, you are automatically in the defense zone and you have to wait for the right opportunity to move through transition and into offense. Against a good doubles team, you may never get that chance. So what is your partner doing up in the offense zone if you can never come up and connect with her?

Finally, if you receive serve and stay back in the defense zone, you may never make it to the offense zone, unless your return is so powerful that it sets up your partner for an easy put-away, your partner is vulnerable up in the offense zone alone and must attempt to come back in defense and help out. The *gap* between the partners is the main thing to protect and defend against.

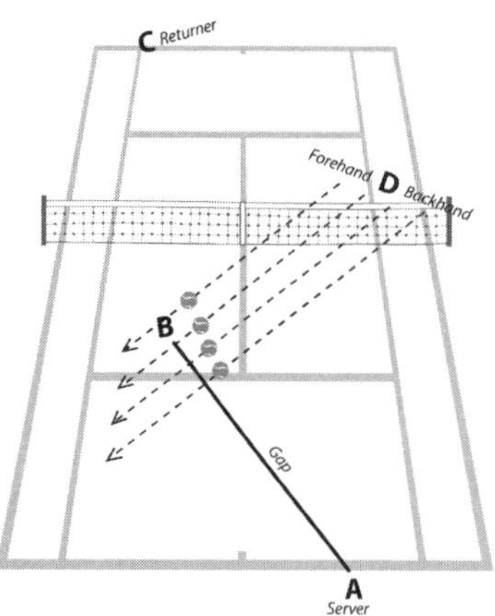

Understand clearly: Your goal is to be able to hit a wining shot between your opponents, to *bisect the plane** between them. If your partner is in the offense zone and you are in the defense zone, there's a huge gap and it offers your opponents an easy target to win a point. Both of you must be thinking of how you're going to get together *as soon as possible* into a major zone, offense zone or defense zone and take charge of the play.

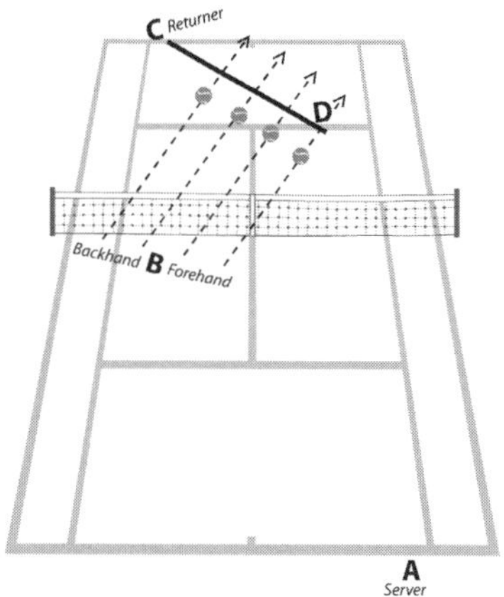

At the same time, as a team is working on getting together in a major zone, offense or defense, the opponents are working hard to keep you separated, preventing you from getting set together in the same major zone. Again, it's no time for panic. With patience and practice, you'll see how it's very much like two-person volleyball.

Yes, volleyball. The essence of the two-person game is that when the opponent is hitting the ball over the net, *both players* know what they must do to block the shot and set up a winning shot. Doubles tennis is the same thing. It seems like a much faster game, but you have

* BISECTING THE PLANE: Imagine a line drawn between your opponents as being the "plane." Your ideal shot should be at a 90 degree angle to that line (perpendicular to it), or as close to 90 degrees as possible, so that the ball bounces in front of that line.

extra tools to deal with the situation—a fast surface to move on and your racquet.

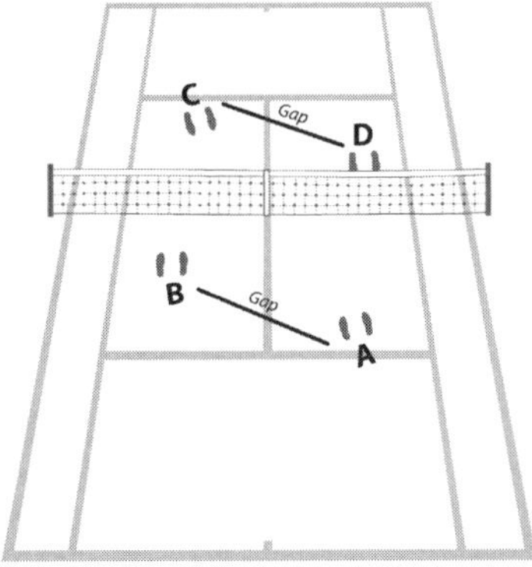

Does the volleyball analogy make it simpler to understand? I hope so. The key is Patience and I know you might be tired of hearing that word, but I bet you probably didn't associate it with your game until now. Stay calm, take your time with your shots, set up the point, don't panic, don't rush. When you're back there in the defense zone, the two things you have going for you are TIME and SPACE. You have lots of each and you must learn to use them wisely.

If you and your partner are in the defense zone, your opponents ought to be in their offense zone. You must stay in defense and play patiently until the invitation comes (in form of a shorter, easier ball) for one of you to move up to the transition zone, hitting either an offensive passing shot down the middle or at the net person or a short sharp angled shot and proceeding to the offense and attack zone, finishing off the point. Your partner stays back in defense, close to the center mark and holds down the defense in case you, her partner, don't get the job done. If she then gets an invitation she can move up and join you. If she does not get the invite but instead is forced back further in defense you then go back again and join her in defense.

If for some reason your opponents are still in defense or even if only one of them is in her defense zone, then both of you can move forward through transition zone up to offense zone by hitting a deep ball back to that player. The depth and speed of your shot will tell you how much time you have. A heavy deep ball gives you more time to get to the offense zone, split-step, read the opponent, and be ready than a flat, short ball.

If both opponents are in offense zone and you come up to transition to hit a defensive shot, then you retreat back to your defense zone and wait for a better ball, an "offensive invitation" from your opponents. Be patient; it'll come.

REMEMBER: The defense zone is huge. There's a lot of court to patrol and unless you're one of those players who enjoys running down balls all day long, you *must* develop the habit of trying to get to the offense zone at every opportunity.

The two major zones are the offense zone and the defense zone and you should always try to be in the same one of those as your partner and be willing and ready to hit lots of shots from either one. Why? No big gap between you.

The two minor (but very important) zones are the transition zone and the attack zone. In these areas, only one of you (you or your partner) should be in at any given time and the reason you're there is to hit the ball—*just once!*

Hit the ball and transition to a major zone—either to your defense zone or offense zone *depending on where your partner is,* which "home" is closest to you, and whether you hit an offensive or a defensive shot.

Write this on your sweatband or say it to yourself before going to sleep at night: "The object of a good doubles team is to be in the same major zone together, at the same time, defense zone or offense zone."

Right now, just take my word for it. In a few minutes, you'll see how this works, how you will control the game, set the pace, win your match. Take it on trust for now and watch doubles matches on television and see how often the winners do exactly by instinct what I'm teaching you one step at a time.

The nice thing about it, remember, is that when you're done, you'll be playing winning tennis, too.

HELLE'S HINTS

Watch a lot of doubles. Notice how the good players consistently play together in the defense or offense zone. It's too bad television doesn't show more doubles play since the majority of players today play this game. However, be patient, with your help, we can and will change that. Yes, we can make a difference.

Maybe there's hope. Thanks to the Jensen brothers, the Woodies, the Williams sisters, and the Bryan brothers and their let's-have-some-fun approach to the game, we may actually begin seeing more doubles on television.

5

LESSON FIVE

the transition zone

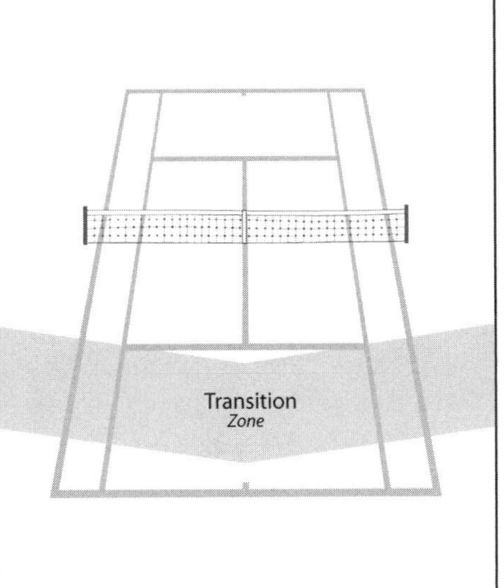

I decided to call this the transition zone because it's a zone where you make the transition to defense or offense. It's been called No Man's (or Woman's) Land by some because it's the place where I see a lot of club players standing around, waiting for something to happen, waiting for their opponents to hit them something to which they can react. I tell my students that when they're doing that, they aren't tennis players, they're *spectators.*

As the name implies, "transition" means you're going somewhere and that's the whole point of this zone. It's a one-shot zone and you either continue through it to offense zone or retreat to the defense zone. You should know before your shot where you are going after you hit the ball. Two choices: offense zone, defense zone.

Don't hit a shot in this area of the court and stand there and watch your handiwork. Get moving one way or the other. *Find your partner!* Since she is not hitting the ball, she can proceed to the appropriate zone, offense or defense, thereby taking charge of the situation and letting the one of you who is hitting the ball know where to move afterwards *and* what shot would be best. The usual picture I see here is a player watching her partner's shot from transition and now both players have to move a lot and chances of not getting ready to read and react before the opponents' next shot are practically guaranteed.

Many times I see one player moving forward to offense and the other back to defense after a shot. The result is total confusion and, as a result, mis-communication and loss of point.

You both must be in a major zone (offense or defense) before your opponent hits the ball. It's best if you're both in the *same* major zone. Don't get separated. Talk to each other. When you and your partner are communicating, you're a unified tennis force out there. Be together and you're going to be winners.

If your partner is in the offense zone, *you* should attempt to get to the offense zone with her. The opposite is also true. If she's in the defense zone and you know she's going to stay there, you should get back to the defense zone with her. A lob is usually a wise shot to give both players time to get together in the defense zone. If you're still standing in the transition zone when the ball you hit has bounced on the other side, you're doing something wrong. (Maybe you're doing nothing at all.) Now it's too late to move. Now you're going to get it. Now you are in trouble. You're standing in the zone where most balls bounce and are an easy target for your opponents. You got caught in the transition zone.

Okay, I can hear you saying it now, "I didn't have time to move to get that shot." And you're right. You didn't have time to move because you froze after you hit the ball *and* you probably hit the wrong shot. The most important time to improve your position, to take command of the situation on the court, is *between the time you stroke the ball and when it bounces on your opponent's court.* If you're not moving then, you have lost your chance and you're playing against the odds.

Notice I said the *bounce* on the opponents' court. This is to give you time to move from zone to zone. If there is no bounce because you hit to the player at the net and she is volleying, you have less time to move after your shot. So remember: Choose a shot that will bounce on your opponents' court when you need to change zones or you need to buy time.

what to hit in the transition zone.

Have a plan, make a decision. **REMEMBER**: Hit the ball from the transition zone and then get out. That gives you some choices and with choices come dilemmas. If you're in Transition Zone Town for one shot, make it a beneficial one. By beneficial, I mean make a shot that will either help your partner and you get into the offense zone or back in the defense zone.

Don't depend on terrific winning shots from here to win your doubles matches. First of all, no tennis player in the world can consistently hit terrific shots. *No one.* Pros don't depend on that strategy. They build up the point to eventually hit a winner to the open court.

What you *can* depend on is your knowledge, your Patience, your ability (along with your partner's) to know what you're going to do, how to set up in your zones, play the odds, build up the point and win the day.

Most first volleys after a serve are hit from the transition zone. You have to become accustomed to that. Most players think they have to get to the service line after their serve. They never make it and get caught with the ball at their feet time after time. What you do is this: After you serve, you push off and run *towards* the service line, following your ball. Slow down and pause when your serve *bounces* in your opponent's service box, so you are ready to make your little split-step/hop as your opponent's racquet comes forward to strike the ball, so you can read and react and move forward to the receiver's return.

YOU GO AS FAR AS YOU CAN. The *bounce* of your serve tells you when to slow down, and be ready to make your hop. After your split-step/hop, you turn and *move again* to get to your opponent's shot. You are ready for anything as long as you paused on the bounce and hopped at the swing of your opponent's racquet. That's usually three-four steps after your serve, depending on the speed of your serve, then split-step, turn and move towards the ball.

HELLE'S HINTS

Practice this move *without* a ball. Execute a service motion, push off and run. Get as far in as you possibly can. After three steps, split-step (the hopscotch move, see "Definitions") and be ready to immediately turn your body for a forehand or backhand volley and move again toward the (imaginary) oncoming ball with lots of little steps. After you've mastered that, practice *with* a ball, but no opponent. Follow your serve in towards the offense zone and split when your serve bounces. Then you have time from the bounce of your serve to your opponent's hit to react, turn, *move* and prepare to hit the volley or half-volley. Your first volley can be hit from the transition zone if the return is deep or if it is so wide you can't get into the offense zone. After the first volley is hit, you can proceed to the offense zone

SPLIT, TURN & MOVE. Turning your shoulder when you see whether it will be a forehand or a backhand. When the ball leaves your opponent's racquet, get on the side of the ball and move to it. MOVE TO VOLLEY. Go to the ball rather than letting the ball come to you when you are volleying. HIT & RECOVER. Regardless of how well you executed your shot, know where you're going to recover to before you hit your shot, and immediately split after you hit and recover with sidesteps toward the recovery location.

6

LESSON SIX

the offense zone

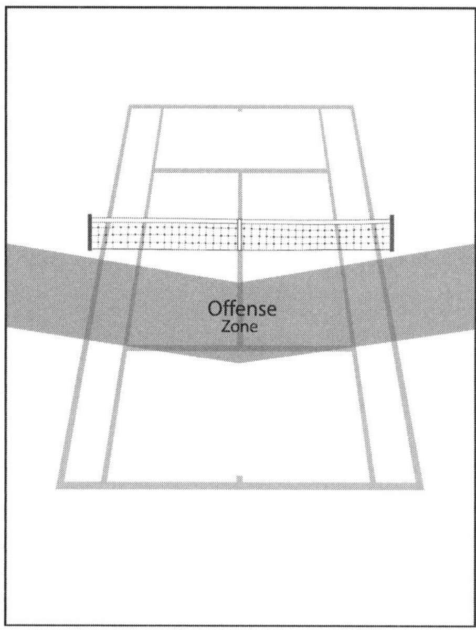

The main goal for you and your partner is to be together in the offense zone and defend against any shot your opponents may hit. When one of your opponents is going to hit the ball, the ideal is for you and your partner to be together in this portion of the court *before* the opponent hits the ball.

Work on recognizing this zone first. Watch some doubles matches, at your club, rec center or even on television, and you'll see how this works to great advantage. Understand, too, that both server and returner have to work to get there and may have to hit several balls before they arrive in the offense zone. Their respective partners are given these positions before the point begins, so they have less work to do.

playing the offense zone.

I don't want to oversimplify, but if you and your partner can both get into the offense zone, the odds are you will win the point.

The offense zone is quite large and it makes a huge difference exactly *where* you and your partner are. I'll get to this in more detail a bit later.

Be aware, one of you may be on or inside the service line and not too close to the net. This allows you the flexibility to get the lob or anything else crosscourt, to hit a volley. Don't over-commit yourself. Take time to assess the situation in front of you. Remember you can *think* a lot faster than you can play, so you have plenty of mental time to keep your options open. A friend of mine likens this to pilots who say they "must always fly ahead of the airplane." That works. I remind you again that tennis is not just a stroking game; it is a thinking game, too. A well-played match exercises your mind as well as your body.

From the offense zone you can come forward and close in for the attack (attack zone) with a put-away volley, or stay where you are for a reflex/defensive volley or you can back up for a deep lob in the transition zone.

TIP: In the offense zone, you should always try to volley every ball, meaning "no bounce." *However,* there are some balls you will have to take as a half volley if you're going to cover 100% of the court. I'll get to this later.

When you're in the offense zone, you need to practice Patience, something many club players don't bring on the court with them. Patience is mental discipline. If you're patient, you can be ready to hit to the *deepest opponent,* (usually crosscourt), avoiding your other adversary who's on top of her offense zone and looking to poach and cut off your shot.

Don't plan on hitting a winner from the offense zone.

Be patient and keep your balls down at the feet of your deepest opponent (usually crosscourt). You have to wait for the right ball to come that will allow you to close-in, by moving to the attack zone and putting the ball away at the feet of your closest opponent.

In adapting to this winning style of play, you have to get your head in the game and keep it there. If you want to talk to yourself, do so, but quietly, please. Opponents may think its a bit odd at the beginning, but when you start beating them regularly, they're going to ask you what it was you were saying to yourself out there.

TIP: The primary goal of a doubles team is always to get into the offense zone as soon as an opportunity occurs. Work toward this, *create* your opportunity because this is where your team can play its most aggressive tennis and at the same time cover the court most effectively and put the most pressure on your opponents.

Remember, the offense zone is the area where most players try to put the ball away AND THAT'S WRONG. It's a little too far from the net and that means you're increasing the odds of hitting the ball either into the net or out of bounds.

This is where you play offense, a lot of it. But be careful of the *kind* of offense you play here. The correct strategy is to set up the point, build toward it, *fly ahead of the airplane*. You need to practice staying in this zone, making fewer and fewer mistakes, practicing capital "p" Patience, waiting for the right shot for you or your partner to close—move forward into the attack zone, where you terminate the point. Close*!* And hit the ball *away* from your deepest opponent.

Okay, okay, I realize you're wondering where you and your partner should be in relation to each other. I'm going to get to that, but for right now believe me, there's a natural flow of things here and let's stick with the plan a little bit longer. H-o-w-e-v-e-r, I'll tell you right now that you and your partner should *never* be on line side-by-side—parallel to the net. Did you get that? Never on line, side-by-side parallel to the net. Not ever*!* A...B Never*!*

using your chart smarts.

Look at the zone chart again. The attack zone is the smallest. It's not very big and from this moment forward, I want you to start believing that when you get into it, you're going to put the ball away for a winner. *Until then, play more patiently in the other zones.*

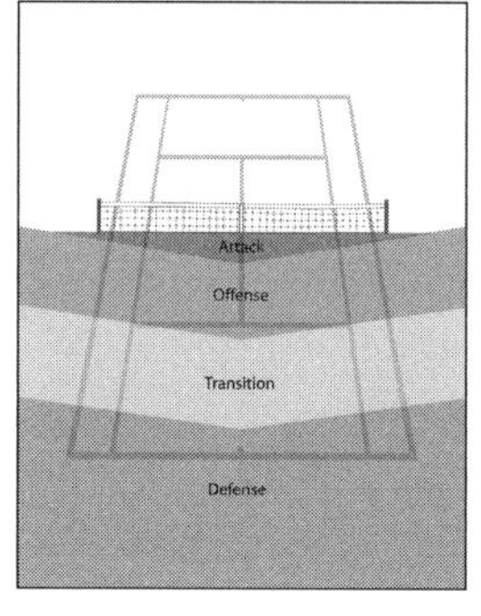

You hit crosscourt and down the middle from the offense zone to the deepest player, to enable your partner to move forward to the attack zone in anticipation and put the ball away towards the closest player, like this:

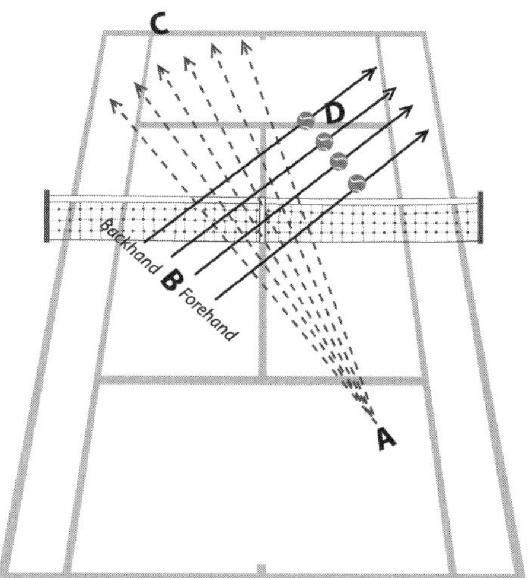

The most common error in doubles occurs when the crosscourt player (server or returner) wants to do it all and tries to put the ball away straight down the line for a winner. It's the correct placement, but the shot should come from your partner in order to get the correct angle on the shot. I call it the *"X" It Out!* The crosscourt player sets up the point by hitting crosscourt. That's one side of an "x." Then the partner can move in, intercept the ball, and angle the next shot, completing the "x."

CAUTION: Don't overrun and end up in attack zone too soon because your opponents have that great defense weapon, The Lob. Bingo, you're off and running again, gritting your teeth and thinking about "forgetting" your club membership dues and giving your tennis racquets to someone you really despise. We'll get to the attack zone soon enough. For now, concentrate on the offense zone because if you really think about it, here's the only region of the court where you can take charge, take control of the game and set up a point for your team.

This book isn't about tennis stroke production, but you must develop confidence in your overhead if you are going to play from the offense zone. When your opponents start lobbing, tell yourself, *Great! Now they're in real trouble.*

They're paying you a compliment and you should thank them with a deadly smash.

CAUTION: If you find that your opponents are consistently effective with offensive lobs, you are closing in too soon and too far. Also, the shot you hit previously did not put enough pressure on your opponent.

HELLE'S HINTS

Build up the point by hitting to the deepest opponent, usually crosscourt, so your partner can be ready to step in and cut off the ball in an angle to complete the X. This is a perfect "One-Two" play, but it depends severely on always hitting to the deepest opponent.

7

LESSON SEVEN

the attack zone

also known as "the killer zone" (think of it as "the one-shot zone")

Listen, this is where everyone wants to be. It's where you look great, you can play hired gun, kill that fuzzy little ball and clench your fist and jab your chin at the sky and know in your heart this is the greatest game in the world.

Which is why too many players spend too much time there.

Think about it. Look at the attack zone. Not much room, close quarters, two partners, two racquets, two opponents, one ball...a lot can happen. But it doesn't. Not very often. We tend to remember our kills and forget the deadly lobs over our heads. It has something to do with how we think about sports in general. Flamboyance is king. Ooops, queen. The great smash, the crisp volley, these things create wonderful pictures in our minds.

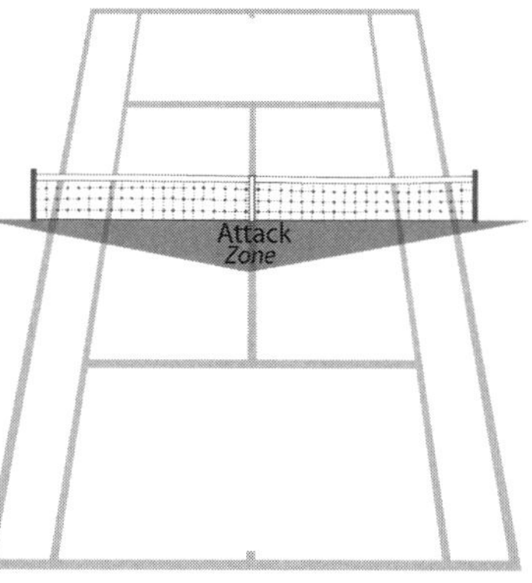

They're what I call Pictures of Victors and I want you to take my warning: "**CAUTION**:

PLAYING IN THE ATTACK ZONE CAN BE HAZARDOUS TO YOUR TENNIS HEALTH."

I don't mean wear and tear on your body parts, I mean the mental game, that thing that gets you out on the court in the first place.

First of all, there are times you should be in the attack zone and there are times you should get the #@%!* out of there. This is a one-shot zone. You move towards the ball and hit *down on the ball from the attack zone*. If you don't put the ball away from here on your first shot, it is very unlikely you'll get another chance. Take your shot and get back into the offense zone just in case the ball does come back and then set up your point again.

TIP: Wait for the ball that allows you *to move into the attack zone* to put it away. If you're in the offense zone, it's your game and you and your partner are working the strategy. Your opponents are running around trying to hit a tennis ball and you're playing ahead of them, *prepared when the opportunity comes to close in for the kill.*

The key, players, is to *MOVE* into the attack zone to hit your shot. Most club players stand here waiting for the ball to come so they can smack it. Lobs over you become more frequent and your poor partner is struggling at the baseline, trying to patrol that huge defense zone by herself, just to keep the two of you in the point. You may hear her huffing and puffing, but you can't hear what she's thinking and it isn't what to get you for your birthday.

To cite the obvious, the closer you are to the net, the less reaction time you have and you're a non-moving target. Another name for the attack zone is the killer zone. No prisoners. Move to the ball—angle it away for the winner, and get back after you hit your shot. It's a one-shot deal, make or break. Even if your killer instinct fails or you don't get a solid hit, it's extremely important to remember that you should take *no more than one hit* in the attack zone and get immediately back to the offense zone. What you have to do is break the habit of standing there, watching your shot.

*And in conclusion...*a few final words about the attack zone.

When you're in the attack zone, the net isn't an obstacle any more, but there's a new one looming in the background—the baseline. Overhitting from the attack zone is one of the most common errors you see on the tennis courts of the world. It's an easy error to understand. You worked hard to get the shot, you're excited, you see the opportunity before you and the point is yours in your mind and you just don't want this one to come back at you so...you hit it into the fence.

The other situation that occurs when you're in the attack zone is your opponent blocks the ball for mere protection and it is right back at you—many times for a winner. The best place to put the shot is between your opponents or angled out of the court, short and wide. The key is that the ball bounces inside the service box and is gone. Another place to aim is at your closest opponent's feet. Either way, you give them a difficult shot and one for which you'll be prepared *because you're back in your offense zone.*

take a break.

Here's a good place to stop for now. Go back and look at the illustrations. *Learn* the zones. They're important and if you play them correctly, they're where you will play winning tennis.

I want to assume that by now you know the zones and what to do when you are in them and when to be there.

In order to make this work in doubles, of course, you both have to know how to move together within the same major zone. To do this, I'll make good on my promise a short while ago and we'll look at "The Diagonal Up & Back System." Well, I had to call it *something*. Yes, it works a lot better than it sounds.

HELLE'S HINTS

The attack zone is a great place to hit from but make sure you hit down on the ball and aim *inside* the service box to avoid overhitting. Angle your shots toward the side fences or hit hard toward the closest opponent's feet. PRACTICE your put-away volleys from here in *really* sharp angles. Your ball should bounce in the service box and hit the side fence before the second bounce. There is great joy in this shot. There's a great challenge, too. Practice hitting the volley in the direction you are moving. *AND* if for some reason you are in the attack zone and are unable to hit *down* on the ball, but have to lift it up over the net, hit the ball to the deepest player in order to buy time for you to return to offense and reset.

8

LESSON EIGHT

the game

I want to take a moment to tell you that I think doubles is just about the best game you could play or watch in your whole life. It can bring you a lot of pleasure. (If not now, *after* you finish this book.) It's a game friends play with and against each other. It's a game of skill that requires you to be able to think and plan as much as stroke the ball and it enables you to derive as much pleasure from outwitting your opponents as from smashing the heck out of the tennis ball, an endeavor that is as limiting as it is single minded.

Doubles has no match as a game of excitement, rhythm, teamwork and satisfaction. And, as some of my friends and students say, it doesn't require a lot of equipment and what you need is easy to carry and always available. Another thing is that if you're a weekend player, you just about *have* to play doubles if you're going to get a court. Many players don't really begin to grasp the significance of doubles as until they approach their mid-thirties. The subtleties of the game, its mental challenge, its complexities, its finesse, its risks and rewards.

> *"...a game entirely of itself."*
> —Helen Wills

I've talked a lot about Patience, haven't I? Well, it's important. I'm writing this "breather" between lessons to make you exercise a little patience before running into the next section and trying to devour it whole. Yes, you can read this entire book in a single sitting, but you're going to get more from it if you take your time, ease into it, learn the material by taking little bites and not trying to consume it at a single gulp.

I stress Patience out there on the court because it's the single most important virtue you probably don't have. You may have a stunning forehand and a world-class backhand, a killer volley, a keen eye and great footwork, but if you're not patient, you can be beaten by "lesser" players. Conversely, if you *don't* have the stunning forehand, world-class backhand, the killer volley, the keenest eye or the greatest footwork, you can *still* beat opponents whose game is a notch or two above yours. How? Patience and smarts, of course.

Patience leads to consistency and when you can anticipate your opponents' moves and strokes, you're on the way to being able to counter them and win the point, the set, the match, the day, the drinks, the dinner, the trophy, the satisfaction.

four parts to patience.

Everything starts when you place your shot. If you serve down the middle, for example, you can anticipate a return down the middle. *Remember, you know this* before *you serve the ball.* Now you can be "looking" for the shot down the middle and not be surprised when it comes.

The next thing Patience will reveal is what kind of tennis your opponents like to play. The more balls you hit, the more balls your opponents hit and the more information they will give you. Everybody has a favorite shot or two or three and a give-away clue or a habit that announces when they are going to use it. Learn how your opponents play and use their own game against them.

While your mind is calm and you are watching the game progress and waiting for your chance, start recording how your opponents position themselves when they are about to hit the ball. Watch their feet, body, arms, racquet. It might seem to you that you're not equipped to analyze these movements, but stick with it because they're not complicated at all and after a bit of practice, you begin to realize in a blink what they're up to.

If you have been able to practice the stopping and split-step exercise I suggested (see "Definitions"), by now you realize that when your ball bounces, you have time to get *set and observe*...your opponents footwork, body movement, racquet, eyes, the works. Believe me, with a little practice you can assimilate enough information in a very short time to make a good decision about what the shot will be and where it will likely be.

There are only three types of shots your opponent can make — lob, drive, or a short-angle dipper. With the knowledge you've assimilated through ❶ placing your shot, ❷ studying the habits and tendencies of your opponents' shots, and ❸ recognizing which shot she is setting up to make, you can go a long way toward making yourself bulletproof out there on the court.

Think about it seriously. Doubles isn't just sweating, hitting, and running after the ball. Doubles is a head game and the smarter you play the better you play. What's that? I said there were *four* parts to Patience and I've only named three? The fourth is for you and your partner to shift position in relation to the ball to defend against the shot that you now have a pretty good idea is on the way. That's what we'll do now. Break's over. Everybody back out on the court.

HELLE'S HINTS

Practice: The split-step drill (see "Definitions"). Hit crosscourt, baseline to baseline (defense zone to defense zone) and be set and balanced at every bounce on the opponent's court and make yourself watch your opponent approach the ball. Make your little split-step/hop as your opponent swings her racquet at the ball, and you'll be reading and reacting appropriately. Do this every time, so you get used to moving after your own shot—watching your opponent's preparation as well as the ball. Concentration begins here*!* Soon you will know exactly when to split-step and be ready to prepare for the next shot.

Listen: Don't go out and try to conquer your tennis doubles world in one day. You can practice watching opponents' setting up when they're playing someone else and then you can begin to watch your opponent's racquet preparation, how they're setting up their feet, whether they're running toward the ball—backwards, forwards, sideways—and where on the court they're hitting from—which zone, defense, offense, transition or attack.

I know, there seem to be an awful lot of things going on at once out there on the court. Sitting here reading this book, it sounds like something that requires extraordinary skill. It doesn't. I can tell you that some of my students seem a little bewildered by it all at first, but after only an hour or so, they seem to "get it" and they become sharp observers overnight.

Be patient with yourself. You're learning things that will become habits and when they do, you won't have to do them consciously because they'll come naturally and your game will move up a level.

9

LESSON NINE

court coverage togetherness... or the end of confusion

In order to play Dynamite Doubles, you and your partner must work as a team. A poor team is made up of two great individual players who don't play well together. Each tries to win the match by herself. No way. No fun.

A good team is made up of two players who are constantly thinking of one another, moving as one, going for high percentage shots and *always* trying to make the best possible shot in order not to set up her partner to be killed, but rather so she can step in and participate by cutting off the shot and terminating the point with a winner.

Ahh, it sounds so easy on paper.

It's tough and one of the reasons, if you stop to think about it, is the fact that the opening for a winner in doubles is so much smaller compared to singles play. So, the *patient* two of you must help each other set up the point so one of you can eventually find an opening and put the ball away. (Think of what they do in beach volleyball—the setup is in their mind from the moment the game starts.)

Well, in order to carry out your game plan, you and your partner must know who is responsible for which shots and who moves where after each shot.

This is the single, most-confusing element of the game to new (and old) doubles players. YET IT IS SO SIMPLE.

I want to solve it for you.

Consider the Obvious.

First of all, the court is bigger than singles. But there are two players covering it, so there is less space available to hit a winning shot. This doesn't mean you have to make perfect shots to win. It *does* mean you must play smarter, play with more patience, play as a team better than your opponents do. To achieve this you must master court coverage as a team. Really good teams are two players who are constantly thinking of one another, moving as a unit, and—*most important of all*—making the best shot possible so that your partner is not set up to be killed.

You can't win a doubles match by yourself and if you try, you're going to run out of partners and find yourself practicing on the wall a lot. Teamwork*!* That good, old-fashioned cry. Okay, you say, I'm willing to work with my partner, just tell me what to do.

Thought you'd never ask.

First of all, beginning right this minute, while you're reading this book and you're *not* out on the court, realize that the biggest mistake you can make in playing doubles tennis is when you and your partner try to cover the same shot. Listen, it isn't just you. Beginners do it, very advanced players do it and even many pros do it. When you think about it, it makes no sense at all for both of you to be trying to cover the same shot. When you're out there in a doubles game, you have to split up and share the duties.

You have to cover as close to 100% of the court at all times when the ball is in the opponents' court. If you can do that, it's going to be next to impossible for them to get a ball through or past you. How do you do that? Think about the zones I've been talking about. *Zones!*

The offense zone is the best, most effective area to be in as a team. When you and your partner are in the offense zone, you are ready for whatever happens. You've won the first phase of the battle by being in the right place at the right time. Now, just stay calm and watch the point begin to unfold. You're in a good place, a safe place, a winning place. You're Positioned, Patient and Alert. Now the questions:

Where is the ball?
Which opponent is going to hit it?
Where are you?
Where is your partner?
What are my responsibilities?
What are my partner's responsibilities?
Which shot are you expecting?
Which shot is your partner expecting?

In Dynamite Doubles you and your partner are **never** side-by-side, parallel to the net. Each of you has different roles and responsibilities, and you're always positioned diagonally from each other.

roles when you and your partner are in offense:

Let's get some action going here. It's the beginning of a point. You're crosscourt from the ball, as the returner is diagonally crosscourt from the server. Just as it is in the offense zone, the crosscourt player is farther back than the partner who faces head-on to the ball. When you are crosscourt from a ball, you have more court to cover than your partner who is in front of the ball—that's why you must be a little bit farther back, so you can cover a bit more court space.

When you turn your body and face the ball, you are turning the whole court with you. Make a V with your arms. That is, hold your arms straight out in front of you and open each arm about 45 degrees to form a V, with your chest at the center. (It doesn't matter if you're right or left-handed.) What you're doing is creating a funnel, a "sphere of influence" your opponent has to hit into. Close your eyes if you want to, but imagine yourself standing on the court facing someone who's going to hit the ball. You have created a funnel—*the lines of which extend from where you stand all the way out to infinity—or to the fences or the net.* Pretend it's just two planes and see the lines going out from your body, covering your court, out-of-bounds, out of town.

Hold that sight line.

If you do, any ball hit to you will come into your funnel. You can cover a sharp crosscourt angled shot or a lob over your partner. You may have to let these shots bounce, but you can get to them before the ball bounces the second time which is when the ball is dead.

There's a visualization trick you can try here. It works for most of my students. After you "see" your position, mentally step over to your partner's position. Take her stance and make another V. Extend that V out to the edge of the universe or wherever. Take a snapshot of the two Vs and what do you have? You have two funnels that cover 100% of your court. And you're both ready to handle whatever comes your way.

Here's what your mental picture should reveal.

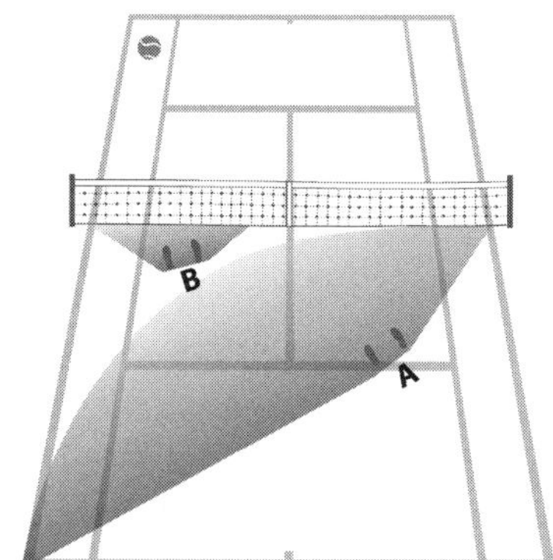

The crosscourt player can extend her arms out a little bit more, to perhaps 140 degrees, since she is covering more of the court.

The close-up player has a slightly narrower V, about 90 degrees as she has less court to cover. Either way, relax your arms, but keep visualizing the funnel they formed.

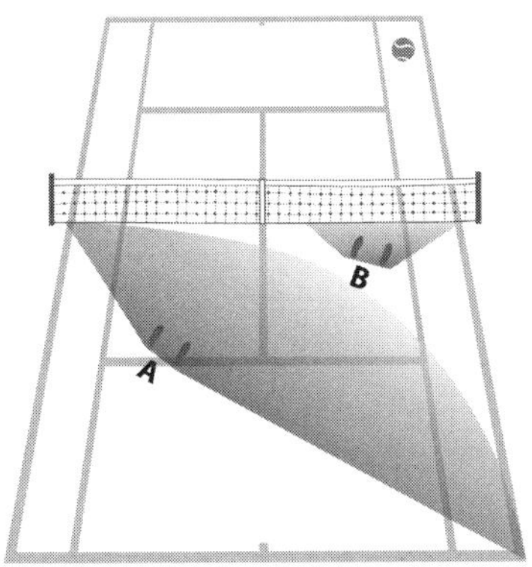

See the coverage here? See the two funnels with both you and your partner armed and dangerous and ready for any shot that comes your way? Notice that the crosscourt player (you) has a wider funnel. As a result crosscourt players have to deal with more shots. That's why I call this member of the team, the workhorse, and believe me, you are. This is another good reason not to be too close to the net. Notice the head-on player (your partner) has a narrower funnel and the result is she has fewer possible shots to contend with—less court to cover—and can therefore be closer to the net and take more chances. She becomes the terminator. Makes great sense, doesn't it? Easy to see when you're sitting in your easy chair, isn't it? Spend a little time *seeing* it and when you get out on the court, it'll be there and you and your partner will know you're "covered."

So there are the roles you and your partner must play in every game of doubles. Now, let's do some role-playing and you just keep moving yourself around in your mind for the moment. It isn't time quite yet to charge out on the court. Although, introduce your partner to the "V" concept the next time you play and she'll be just a step or so behind you.

up and back the diagonal way.

During the course of a tennis point, the ball goes back and forth over the net. (Bet you knew that.) Well, with this vast knowledge, add to it the fact that each time your team changes the direction of the ball, each of you must also change position in order to be ready for the next shot. I'm going to say it again: Don't stand there and admire your great or your terrible shot, get moving either up to become the terminator or back to become the workhorse. Stay in the major zone. Don't leave it. Your V also changes so you're always facing the ball.

The workhorse is *always* DIAGONALLY positioned from the ball on the opposite side of the net. Therefore the workhorse should be responsible for any crosscourt or down the middle shots, as well as all lobs (except for the ones the terminator can reach with an overhead). *The only shot the workhorse cannot possibly take is a drive down the line.* Obviously, your partner's responsibility is to take drives down the line.

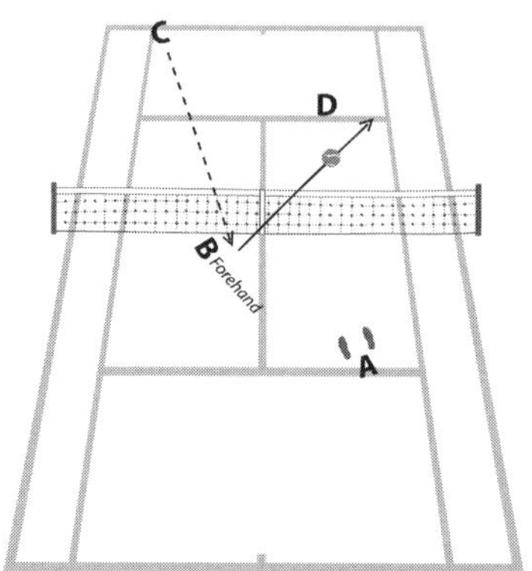

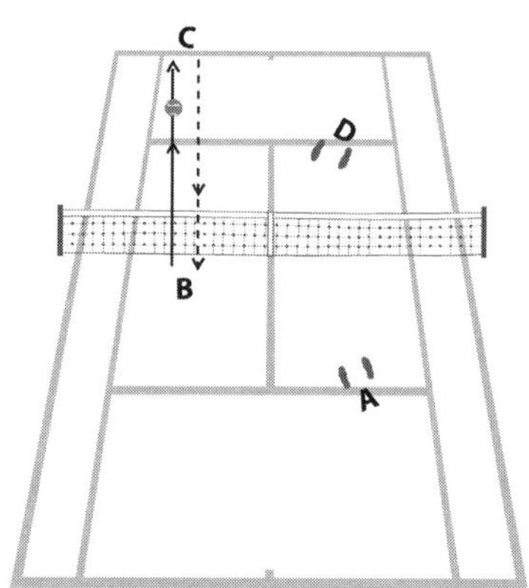

The role of the workhorse is to set up the point, to keep the ball crosscourt toward the opponent's feet so her partner can possibly intercept the ball (poach) and put the ball away ideally by changing the direction of the ball 90 degrees Here's another ball in play:

workhorse A serves. workhorse C returns crosscourt to Server A. Player D moves forward with C's return and becomes the terminator, looking to poach or cut off the next shot from A. C and D have a 50-50 chance of winning the point and have maintained their roles, while challenging the patience of Server A.

If C returns straight ahead at B instead of crosscourt, D now automatically becomes the workhorse. D does not move forward with C's return, but rather, takes a step toward the middle T, pivots, and faces B, ready for any shot. B has two options, depending on the strength of C's return. If C's return is relatively easy, B should change direction of the ball and angle it away.

If C's return is very strong, B ought to block it back defensively toward C, keeping her team in their correct positions. B remains the terminator and her partner A remains the workhorse.

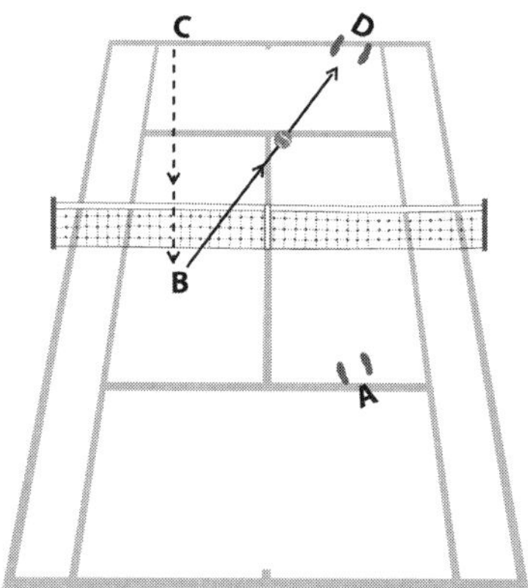

In a case where C is consistently hitting to B and B is terminating and hitting through D, then D ought to start the point back on the baseline with C, in order to have a better chance to retrieve B's shot.

WORKHORSE'S NOTE:
You should always be able to see your partner in front of you when

hitting crosscourt. If not, change direction and make your partner the workhorse, since she is behind you.

Okay, I'll admit this kind of movement requires a lot of alertness on your part. It doesn't take long to realize that changing the direction of the ball is not always the best thing to do. However, this is where average players fail most often. Reaction time is slow (you're watching the shot instead of moving) and the sad result is a gap between you and your partner that is huge and easy for your opponents to hit. Think how many times this has happened to you. Begin today to create a partnership that lets you both know how to avoid that gap and thus the easy put-away by your opponents who are beginning to think they're Venus and Serena.

To continue, when you change direction of the ball from crosscourt to a long line shot you and your partner must not only switch roles and positions, but also—ideally—get into the same major zone. This takes a lot of time and effort. Remember you must always face the opponent who is hitting the ball. When I change direction on a return of serve for example from crosscourt to down the line, I usually hit a lob—to give me and my partner more time to ① get into our new positions and ② get clear on our new roles. I get to the offense zone as the new terminator with my partner who is now the workhorse, anticipate a lob in return, so we get to hit our strong overheads and force our opponents to their defense zone, avoiding any quick put-away by them. Common sense.

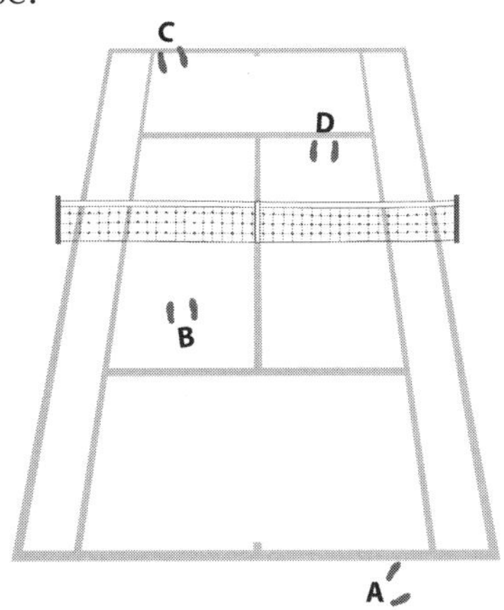

Let's start with the basic doubles position. These positions are standard and most teams start out a match in these positions. This is easy to remember: Try to maintain these relative positions at all cost. The main thing is that you always divide the responsibilities whether you're the aggressive terminator or the patient diagonal workhorse. One of you must keep thinking "Move forward and attack!" and the other, "Be consistent, keep the ball in play, back up my terminator partner." This all happens in the major zones, offense or defense.

This way your team won't lose a point by a lob going over your heads and you both think your partner was going to take it, since you know beforehand that it is the diagonal crosscourt player's shot. With this system, if you go over the points again, you can see you have the lob covered even if you couldn't predict it was coming.

This is the core of Dynamite Doubles: it can make a player who is not moving as well as others, a top class doubles player, and totally confuse the ordinary singles player who only knows how to cover for herself.

It's strategy, it's anticipation, it's patience. It's consistency, it's success and it's FUN. This is what makes it so challenging to play the system. Winning or losing becomes secondary and this allows you to stay in the present, focused on the task right in front of you, playing your best tennis and "letting it happen." My experience is that I win a lot more matches when my focus is on playing the system, *playing the ball on a different level "in the moment"* and not wasting concentration or energy on worrying about winning or losing the match, an event which is beyond that each particular "moment."

Now about more role-playing. Curtain going up*!*

HELLE'S HINTS

Never be side-by-side with your partner, parallel to the net.

The head-on terminator covers down the line line-drives and the short lobs. The workhorse, diagonally across from the ball covers the rest: down the middle shots, all crosscourt shots, lobs and angles ... plus ALL surprises. Easy.

> **Terminator note**: An exception to the rule. When opponents are in charge and shooting bullets at me and my partner when we're in the offense zone, our terminator is not in great condition, she should simply attempt to block the ball back without changing direction. She cannot possibly think about terminating the ball, so she just gets the ball back to the deepest player. In this case, she is keeping the point alive and keeping her team in the correct positions ready for the next shot.

Yes, if you've figured this out, it means she's actually playing defense in the offense zone, a great strategy at times.

10

LESSON TEN

role playing

server/workhorse.

Your role as server is simple: GET YOUR FIRST SERVE IN! Consistency and placement are the most important things on which you must concentrate.

As server, you're the only player who has to start the point from behind the baseline. It's a rule. It also means you're the person on the court who is the farthest from the net. So where do you want to put the ball?

Serve up the middle T. It's your best percentage shot for doubles. Your opponent has very little angle on you *and* your partner can poach (cut off) the return easier. Most returns will come back down the middle when you serve down the middle. Watch some doubles games and see how often that's true. Right away you're mentally ahead in the game because you know that based on your middle T service, the odds are in your favor that the return will be ...down the middle. It can be low or high. Your partner takes the low one. You, the server, take the high one. Great play!

Ideally, Server, you should serve and volley in order to get in the same major zone (offense) as your partner. Since you must begin from behind the baseline, you have two shots to get to the offense zone—first your serve and second your volley or half-volley from the transition zone. By then you'll have arrived in the offense zone, ready to play the rest of the point. A well-placed deep spin serve allows you to come closer to the offense zone for your first volley than if you hit a flat, short serve.

Okay, server/workhorse, after your serve, you have to be prepared to hit the next shot since a high percentage of returns come back crosscourt. This is a difficult shot, so try to get as far into the transition zone as you can before the return is hit. (Remember your split-step practice *without* the ball, then *with* the ball and no opponent, and finally with an opponent? Now is when that pays off. You've gone in as far as you can, paused when your ball bounced and now you're taking in your opponent's moves toward the ball.) Now watch her move to and hit the return, hop as she hits the ball, and react/turn and move for the ball with either a volley or half-volley, depending on what kind of return it is. Try not to kill the first volley. The split-step allowed you to slow down and be balanced and to move forward to the volley or half-volley, with a well-placed, controlled, crosscourt shot. That's all you need to do. And all you *should* do. Your role is to help set up the point. Emphasis there: HELP. Now then, place your volley toward your crosscourt opponent's feet. Ideally, your volley should land just in front of her feet so she can't volley it, but has to dig it out and lift it with a half-volley.

Listen, it's important you know where the crosscourt player is. Is she back on the baseline? Is she in her transition zone? Is she in her offense zone? Take that mental snapshot and *know* where she is because your placement of the volley depends on her location.

After you have hit your first volley, recover quickly into the offense zone, pause when the ball bounces, face your opponent and the ball, and be ready for your hop again as her racquet starts to come forward. You have played your role perfectly and you've achieved your first goal.

Remember, your role is *NEVER, NEVER* to be a spectator, so start moving after you hit the ball, and watch your opponent who is going to hit the ball—don't stand there and watch your shot land in or out. After every shot I hit I ask myself, "When and where do I have to make my next split-step?"

Now the diagonal system I mentioned in the last chapter comes into play. Your partner is in front of you and her role/responsibility is to ① cover the drive down the line, ② look to intercept the crosscourt with a poach, depending on the quality of my first volley, and ③ to take the short lob. Expect her to move up a bit further, close to the attack zone, straight at her opponent. She is the terminator.

You, server, are the crosscourt player or workhorse. (You volleyed back crosscourt after your serve) and you have the larger area of the court to cover. Yes, you have the larger "V," hence the larger funnel for your opponents to hit into. This means you should NOT over-commit, but stay a little behind your partner and wait and see what comes.

If you do this, you'll be ready for ① any crosscourt shot (a drive, a short, sharp-angled dipper or a lob or, ② a down-the-line lob over your partner. That's a lot of responsibility, so don't expect or try to win the point yet. (Patience and consistency. You win more points/games/matches with these two commodities than with anything else and if you're tired of hearing that now, wait until we're finished.)

Your role in this situation is to get the ball back over the net with a placement shot. Your partner, however, may be able to get involved in a poach if your volley penetrated the crosscourt opponent and put her in trouble. You are working toward getting your partner in the attack zone (you non-selfish, good partner you) and she can slip up there when your crosscourt workhorse opponent is in trouble and can barely get the ball back. Keep in mind that you are not always going to be the patient workhorse; try to think of the times when you are going to be the terminator.

If your partner anticipates that your opponent's return is going to be weak—and might be poached—she may step inside the attack zone ...anticipating the weak shot. If so, you must stay back (on the borderline of the offense and transition zone) and cover the potential lob or extreme angle crosscourt. Give your partner the green light and make her look good.

If an extreme angle crosscourt or a great down the line lob comes, you may have to let the ball bounce in order to get to it, and then rebuild your point, but you backed up your partner who had a chance to put the ball away. You have kept the point going and therefore you still have a claim on it. One or two more shots and your partner may find another opportunity.

Think about that. Your role as server has put you in charge of setting the tempo of the game, of playing positively and aggressively, but always in control. If you do not see a clear opportunity to win the point, you push your Reset button and start again. This will give you a sense of being in charge and just that little edge will help your game immeasurably.

Let's go back for a moment. Suppose you *didn't* hit crosscourt, but straight down the line on your first volley. Now your team is in a spot of trouble, as the Brits say. The ball is coming back (*always* expect the ball to come back) and both of you are out of position to make a good return. Immediately, if not sooner, your partner wishes to be behind you. She may take a step toward the middle in anticipation of the shot, but usually the point is over when you hit the ball straight down the line. Either you made a winner or a mistake or your opponent volleyed back for a winner. You were playing singles for a moment and didn't think of your partner or of the consequences of that shot. Low percentage play. It will work at times, but don't count on it as your bread-and-butter shot.

However, all this is a lot of work and you can avoid it *if you just go crosscourt with your first volley.* Remember, crosscourt also means down the middle.

TIP: Sometimes you can get a little mixed-up or lost when you're trying to play these points in your head. I found one of the best ways to work it out is to have you and your partner stand up (even in the living room if necessary) and walk through the points, the two of you narrating the play-by-play.

One of my couch potato football fans tells me that every play in the NFL starts out on a chalkboard and then moves to walk-through stage long before it's ever brought to the practice field, let alone the playing field.

This may help—even if you do it alone. Stand up! Walk and talk your way through the point. Sitting on your duff and reading instructions about how to play your role and trying to keep track of the bouncing ball is possible, but why not stand, walk, point, talk, move.

Try it! Very soon you'll see and feel the diagonal moves within the zones.

HELLE'S HINTS

Go to the tear out pages in the back of this book to find the blank court drawings and draw out that game, point by point. You'll see what a terrible idea it is to go down the line. Always tell your partner in advance if you plan to return down the line to give her a chance to close the gap between you. That lets her know she's to be the workhorse crosscourt player, not the terminator. She can switch hats and anticipate.

Use down the line drive returns rarely and consult with your partner before you do it. It is a very low percentage shot, an all or nothing shot, rather selfish shot and you had better be sure it is the right time to go for it. Know your role, when to play it and when to change it.

11

LESSON ELEVEN

an overview: playing some points

The players I see who indeed do think in terms of serve and volley usually have just those two shots in mind, the Serve and the Volley. That's okay, but the ball better still be in play after those two shots. If you want to put the first volley away, remember what you're doing. In case you don't know, what you're doing is putting an awful lot of pressure on yourself and as a result, a lot of times the serve doesn't even get in because you're one worry ahead of yourself.

Take a deep breath, think of yourself as a workhorse who has to hit a minimum of two shots: Serve and Volley or half-volley (or a ground stroke if you are not coming to the net.) And remember, YOU'RE JUST STARTING THE POINT. Once you've survived these two shots, your odds start getting better and you can start thinking/planning ways to win the point.

Startling things begin to happen when you plan your game this way. One of the early effects is that your opponents most likely won't like to play this way and as a result they'll begin helping you by over-hitting and rushing their shots. On the other hand, if your opponents like this style of play, you must stay alert and be even more patient and you will have a great game with a lot of good points. Find a way to get your terminator partner involved. Make her look good.

another look at serving.

Remember, server, your job is to get up into the offense zone with your partner. Follow your serve in and make your split-step in the transition zone. This will allow you to proceed forward diagonally to volley or half-volley from either the transition or offense zone. After this shot you should recover and be balanced with a split-step in the offense zone. The point is that you end up in the offense zone after your first volley or half-volley. Most players think they have to get to the service line after their serve, and that is what kills them. They never make it quite far enough up and keep on getting beat with the return to their feet. You will make your first split step in the transition zone and then move to the return for the first volley wherever it comes. Your goal as server is to be in the same major zone—offense zone—with your partner after your first volley or half-volley. Your partner should start in the offense zone, NOT in the attack zone so she can be flexible and not be over-committed for the return. She can either close in to attack or go back a step or two to hit an overhead smash.

Neither of you should try to hit winners or to kill the ball from the offense zone. Well-placed, controlled shots are what you need here. Keep your balls crosscourt and down the middle towards the deepest player, making your ball bounce in front of your opponent. If this isn't the way you're playing now, it may seem a bit strange, but I have a story that will show you the percentage plays and explain why this is your best shot selection.

learning then; remembering now.

When I was a Junior Player in Denmark, playing doubles in a division above my age, I had this one point that I still remember vividly.

I served a smashing serve from the deuce court down the middle T. The return popped up and as I came rushing "up to net" (I didn't know about the zones then), I got ready for the ultimate forehand volley winner—right down the line at the net person ahead of me.

I made the shot and thought I had arrived as the greatest doubles player ever. What actually happened was I won the shot and lost the match. Since then I have tried to duplicate that play/shot many times, only to my disappointment and frustration to find out that it did not always work. Actually, that it worked very seldom. I either hit it long—into the net—wide, or quite often right at the player's racquet, which in return blocked the ball back between me and my partner for a winner.

I couldn't figure it out. Nor could I figure out why I had a hard time finding or keeping partners—until...Then one day by accident, I hit that same high volley back crosscourt and the point developed beautifully and some sense of teamwork popped into my mind. Since that day of discovery, I made it a point to promise myself that no matter how tempting that high volley looks, I must stay patient and unselfish and hit it crosscourt towards the middle T at least once.

It has made all the difference in the world to me as a doubles player and to this day I can tell you that when I do see that same shot, I am tempted to repeat the shot I made as a Junior, but now I have the discipline to go along with the percentage play, for now I know that if I get a chance to do it later on in the same point, my chances are greater that I will make it then.

The other point to my story, of course, is that you must never stop learning the game. You owe it to the sport and to yourself to try and become the best player possible.

It doesn't hurt to remember mistakes; often it helps. In actual play, of course, there are a lot of times when you will merely block the balls back with volleys and stay alive that way. Other times your opponents will try to get you away from the net by lobbing the ball, so you must be ready for that as well. Play patiently until you or your partner gets a chance to move forward to the attack zone and terminate the point by hitting the ball in the direction of the closest player and away from the deepest player.

Volleys and overheads do not need to be put-aways. They are regular shots just as ground strokes are, but a lot of players feel that high balls over their head on the fly must be winners. You probably realize you hit a lot of "fly balls" this way.

One of the saddest plays on any court is when one partner has hit an unbelievably great shot and there seems to be almost no chance the ball will come back over the net and they both become spectators. But then the shot does come back and neither of them is ready for it. That is the precise reason I concentrate more on being ready for the next shot than on killing the shot I'm making now. Doubles tennis is full of flashy players who attempt the killer shots, take their Andre Agassi or Serena power shots and anguish when they miss or lose the point on the return. These players often look good on the court, but they can consistently be beaten by the team who makes the fewest mistakes and the highest number of high-percentage shots. One or two good shots in a set doesn't begin to match the feeling you get when you create and execute an artful and winning strategy by stringing a whole series of thoughtful points together.

let's play some points on paper.

Server A and partner B, here we go. SERVE*!*

Server A runs forward *immediately after hitting the serve* (and NOT after she sees whether it is In or Out or how good it is) and pauses when the ball bounces in the service box, ready to split step as the ball is struck by the returner. She will be in the top part of the transition zone by now.

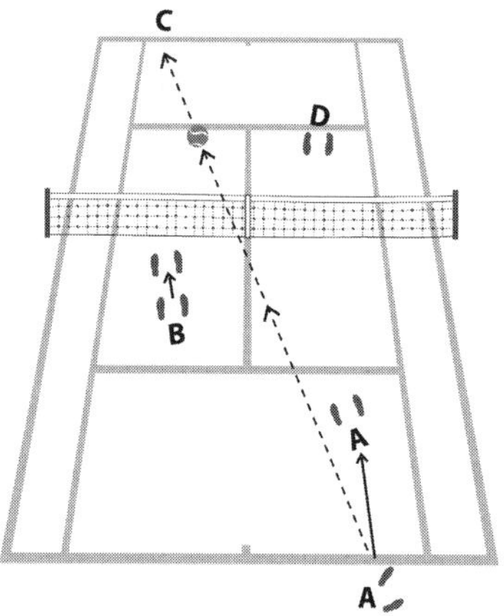

Partner B moves forward toward the attack zone border when she hears her server hit the serve and pauses, ready for her split step hop when the serve bounces in the service box. She is anticipating a shot from C which will allow her to poach (cut off the ball) and place it between C and D for a winner. She must be in the attack zone to do this effectively. This is not a large move—one step up, split-step. Now the return from C goes back crosscourt toward server A. Partner B did not get the ball and moves back in the offense zone—one step back, balance, ready position.

Server A volleys from the transition zone back crosscourt toward the feet of opponent C/returner.

FREEZE FRAME*!*

Server A, where should you be now? **ANSWER**: In your offense zone, inside the service line, facing the ball and opponent C in a "V" angle.

Partner B, what's your move? *[Remember, B has moved two times so far. One: forward when A served, two: back one step as C returned to A.]* **ANSWER**: One step up, facing ball and C, ready to close.

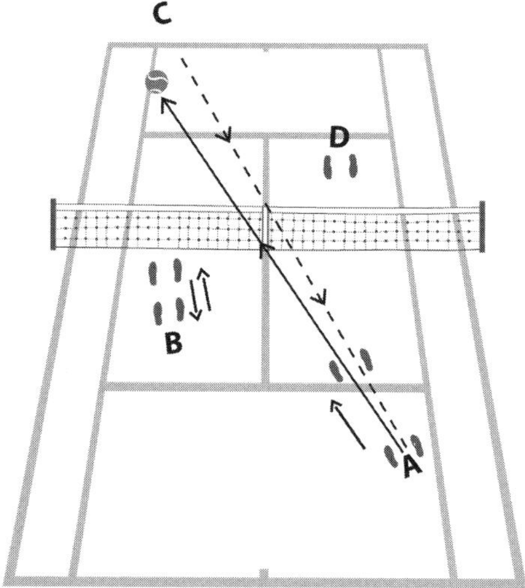

See how A and B are positioned relative to each other? This is the very beginning of Dynamite Doubles Winning Tennis b-e-c-a-u-s-e you and your partner always know where to position yourselves *in relation to the ball in your opponents' court and in relation to each other.* MAKE SURE YOU UNDERSTAND THIS.

Remember what you've learned so far: Each player must think in terms of offense and defense *within the same major zone,* and each player's role changes *when they change the direction of the ball.* It

ALWAYS depends on where the ball is. Hey, it's a BALL game!

Until now, as a club doubles player, the chances are just about 100% that you have been more involved with executing your shots and beating your opponents than you have with getting into position to defend your court against opponents' shots. You probably have too many concerns about avoiding great shots from your opponents—rather than concentrating on a 100% defense by your team against those shots. Remember, if you are constantly ready and in the correct position for the most likely shot coming from your opponents, you can ANTICIPATE the oncoming shot and BE READY for it. This way even the very best executed shot by your opponents will be covered by you and your partner.

Honestly, this will take some time in the beginning because you're looking at the game differently. Some of my students seem to fight this for a while, but after they spend some time and begin to see how this basic wisdom is winning points, games and matches for them, it all begins to make sense. In fact, many of them tell me they can't believe they haven't *always* thought about doubles tennis this way!

My belief and the system I'm teaching you in this book is based on the simple premise that the better, smarter, more intelligent shot you hit, the more likely you can cover 100% of your court for the next shot and that you and your partner can split the roles and duties between you, keeping the ball in play until you can go for the winner or until your opponents lose their cool and go for the impossible or low percentage shot.

net affinity.

It's difficult to keep yourself away from the net, the attack zone, whether you're the workhorse or the terminator. What happens *so often* is that you and your partner both end up in the attack zone, closing in for the kill...and your opponent lobs you.

On the other hand, if you both hang back on the service line or behind it, expecting a lob, what happens if they hit a low drive down the line, down the middle, or sharp-angled? I'll tell you what happens (you already know): Neither of you can get to the ball and the eyes of you and your partner start throwing sparks and/or the two of you get a bit deranged, wondering how you could get beat like that.

Either way, this makes for a ragged, frustrating, non-managed game that makes you wonder why you're doing this to yourself. You may even start thinking about looking for a new partner about now. Hey, that's not the plan! Doubles ought to be a lot of fun and you ought to take great pleasure in establishing and controlling the pace, making your shots, playing for your opportunities, maintaining your unbreakable team spirit and winning *more* than your share of points. You shouldn't be playing tennis to punish yourself. You ought to take great joy in your game and glory in your team's consistency and winning ways.

Remember, you get the same score whether you hit the winner or your opponent hits the fence. Play the odds. Accept this simple fact: You will lose points and never play a perfect game. Understand this and you free yourself from the guilt of not playing perfectly and instead enjoy the process of winning points, games, sets, matches. Stay in the present, focus on the moment, play one point at a time to the best of your ability. Do this and I promise good things—and good tennis times—will follow.

back to the court.

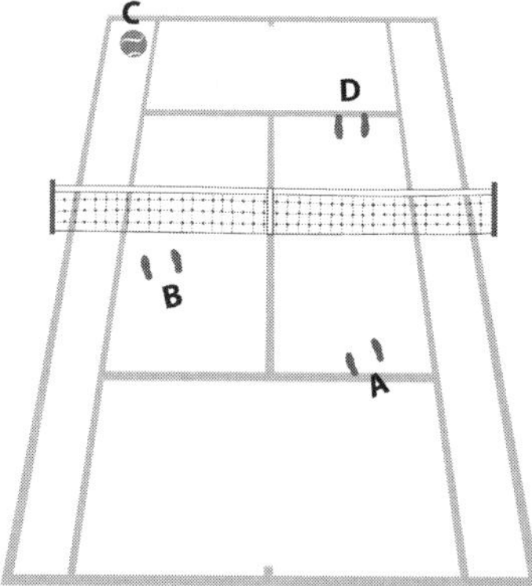

Dividing and playing your roles gives you court coverage that can drive your opponents crazy. Let's say you [A] and your partner B are in the offense zone and opponent C is still in her defense zone, at the baseline, just about to hit the ball.

In this illustration, it's obvious that if player B (your partner) positions herself a little ahead of you [A], she is thinking in terms of wanting the ball from C and now she becomes the terminator. She has a better chance to put the ball away and is nearer to C and the ball and can get there quicker than you A can. You, A, are *diagonally across* from the ball and you assume the role of workhorse, taking care of most overheads and anything crosscourt that attacker B doesn't want.

B's role is to be hip to opportunities. (My one bad pun, I promise.) Anyway, B should try to tempt C to make a down-the-line passing shot. B's right hip (position) protects the middle T and opens up the alley slightly...which is B's responsibility anyway, as well as a shot C generally loves to try. And when I said tempt, I mean it. You really want to bait those guys on the other side of the net. *Position is everything.* You are not necessarily there to hit the middle ball. (Really.) You are there to be in the way of opponent C's view for the winner down the middle. Turn your back slightly to your partner and to the T, face C and look for the down-the-line only! B, you don't want to get beat down the line, but don't stand in the alley to avoid it, either. Tempt your opponent, she can't read your mind, only your body language.

crosscourt continuity.

It's beginning to dawn on you, perhaps, that the name of the game in doubles is "Crosscourt" and if you can make this shot consistently, you are getting to be a seasoned doubles partner. I know, you know, we all know how tempting it is to look really good by trying to nail that net woman down the line or volley right at her. We can grunt and hit and look good and smash that old ball around and isn't that what tennis is all about?

No.

Sure it's easy to remember how good we looked going for the big, game-winning hit, the power and the glory of feeling like one of the pros we watch on television, but the real truth of the matter is that we forget how many times when we're playing that way that we hit the net, the fence or her racquet and lost the point that was such a winner in our minds before we played it.

So go crosscourt towards your opponent's feet and let her hit up at the shot so your partner can intercept and put the ball away. You make her look good (if she makes it) and you have a partner who wants to play with you the next time.

Doubles can be an extremely rewarding team effort or it can be frustration and bitterness. The thing about Dynamite Doubles is that you'll be smiling at the end of the game and planning who you'll beat next time.

HELLE'S HINTS

Best Doubles Drill. Practice crosscourt relentlessly so you don't get impatient and go down the line too early and for the wrong reason. Mix it up though by practicing hitting short or deep into the crosscourt area, wide-angle into the alley, or down the middle. Slice or topspin, hard or soft. Practice from the defense zone and work your way through transition to offense, and make the split-step hop every time before your opponent hits the ball. Every time you have the urge to go for the down the line shot, hit with power to the middle T instead.

Crosscourt translates to control, your control of the game.

12

LESSON TWELVE

Fred & Ginger doubles

We're all familiar with the observation that "Ginger Rogers danced every step Fred Astaire danced—backwards and in high heels." The real truth of their successful partnership was the smooth and coordinated way they danced together, seeming to make it up as they went along. Compare this to ballroom dancing where couples are smiling, executing intricate steps and turns, but there's an unnatural rigidity and there doesn't seem to be as much joy. I'll take the Fred and Ginger way every time.

Especially on the tennis court.

When you play doubles, it's important, no, it's crucial how you and your partner match up together—the way you move together on the court and the shots you chose to hit. That's what your opponents see. What they *don't* see is even more important, because it's what makes you better than they are. And what they don't see is the attitude and respect you and your partner have for each other, a mutual *trust* and an unwritten agreement of responsibility-sharing. This all-important mental part of the game distinctly affects your physical game. If you and your partner are in tune mentally, the chances are 100% that you'll enjoy yourself, play better, and probably do much better than you expected.

Just as dancers must be "in sync" so it is with doubles partners. It's even more important because you're engaged in a contest against opponents who may be faster or stronger or more powerful hitters than you, but if they're not working together, you can—and should—beat them.

moving together on the court.

Remember, never side-by-side, parallel to the net, but always a little staggered so one player is slightly ahead of the other, depending on which opponent is hitting the ball, with both of you facing in the direction of the ball.

When you and your partner are in the same major zone offense or defense, the crosscourt player is always a little behind her partner and facing the ball in a "V" angle, creating that "sphere of influence" that's irresistible. The terminator, the partner closest to the ball, creating her own "V," her sphere of influence that's irresistible. Each of you is watching the ball and your opponent who is getting ready to hit the ball very closely and you are both ready for the ball *and in a position to get to it.* If you're the terminator, you're thinking "*Terminate, close-in.*" If you're the workhorse, you're saying to yourself, "*Defend at any cost against a drive, a lob or the angle crosscourt.*" Remember your "V"...opponents are hitting right into your funnel.

You have control of the game now, but if you and your partner don't move together in a system that allows you to keep control, your opponents will be able to separate you, to bisect the plane between you and begin to get you confused and out of position, out of balance, out of sync.

The best way to prevent this, recall, is that you and your partner always move *right after either of you has hit a ball.* You move while the ball is in flight to a new position that allows you to be ready for the next shot from your opponents. Remember, too: You pause and watch the opponent who is going to hit the ball when the ball bounces on their court, regardless of where you are on the court. If there isn't going to be a bounce, because your opponent is going to volley it, then pause when your ball clears the net, and split-step/hop as she strikes the ball.

As you grow into this system, you will find that during a point you will move quite a bit—whether forward, backward, diagonally or on the spot. One of you has just hit the ball and you both move. Hey, you're dancing and the cue to move is when the ball is in your court and one of you hits the ball. If both of you don't move when the ball is traveling across the net from your side, then you're doing something wrong and you're on your way to losing your position, control and, eventually, the point.

Where do you go?

That depends on where the ball is going. You position yourself in relation to which opponent is going to hit the ball. Most club players stand, their feet in concrete, to see if the ball is In or Out before they take that first step towards recovering. Your opponent will tell you whether she is playing it or not. Watch her and you will know whether to keep playing or not. Instead of admiring your stroke ("spectating"), I think you can *always assume* the shot is going to be in and get in position for the return. Hit the ball and recover to your next spot.

Okay, Helle, where's my next spot? Can you read minds?

No, but then you don't have to

in doubles. If you hit crosscourt, then you know by now that you stay behind your partner, who takes a step forward to be in front of you and closer to the opponent who is about to hit the ball. In the beginning, you may not think you have time to get in position before your opponent returns the ball. Not true. You have *plenty* of time, IF you begin to move the instant the ball is hit from your side of the net.

REMEMBER: Face the ball. Look at the court as if it had no lines. As Zen-like as this sounds, it *will* expand the boundaries of your doubles game.

TIP: The less you change direction of the ball, the less you have to move. The formula: Crosscourt = Less Movement = More Time to Anticipate = Smart Play.

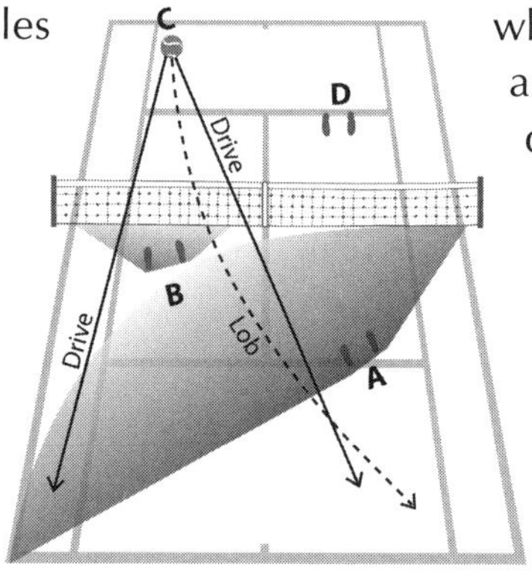

forcing the issue & moving with purpose.

Your position forces your opponents to hit certain shots. You don't always move so you can get the ball, but instead, to force opponents to avoid you—making it possible for your partner to get it. This is important, so let me explain it a bit more.

When my partner closes in after I have hit crosscourt, our opponent sees that and wants to avoid my partner. So what does she do? She either lifts the ball up or tries to hit more crosscourt. I can handle those two shots. It's the low line drive down the middle at the T that may get me, so my partner helps tremendously by *closing in*. (Where'd you think the name "Close" came from?) If our opponent does not lift the ball, or if she does not go crosscourt, she may try for the winner down the line—the shot my partner is waiting for.

Note how you [B] are *baiting* the opponent [C] who's always looking for an opening for her down-the-line shot. You're protecting the T with your right hip and making C hit either down the alley —which you are ready for with a backhand (for righties)—or forcing C's shot up and over, going towards A, which is Christmas morning for her. Or: make C hit wider, more crosscourt and A loves this wide volley even more. Pretty neat, hey? Also drives your opponents slightly crazy.

Now, don't just move for motion's sake, move where you're supposed to and where you're supposed to move is determined by where the ball lands on your opponent's court. It's *crucial to follow the flight of the ball* as well as watching your opponent, so you'll be able to get in position, face the opponent who is hitting the ball, and be Ready to Read and React.

You and your partners must practice moving together after each hit, and be balanced and ready to split-step/hop in your respective positions by the time the ball bounces. This way you have a little time before your opponent's actual hit to Read the situation, React to whatever your opponent decides to do.

Look again at the width of the "V" which shows you the court area that's your responsibility. Note, again, there is no space between you and your partner's coverage. It doesn't take long for your opponents to become pretty frustrated when they find you closing the gap they saw open just a second ago. Furthermore, you're challenging them every time to come up with a really great shot. After a couple of games, you'll find they're rushing their shots and going for low percentage shots. Most people think it's wrong to hit a ball an opponent can get to. It's always okay to hit a ball the crosscourt workhorse can get. Better that than making an error. The irony of that kind of thinking is that you can hit balls to the feet, to the body, to the weakness of the workhorse, that make them struggle, that put them off their game. Voilà! You're in charge! Play smart, play Dynamite Doubles and you'll *stay* in control of the game.

Wrong-way Wanda! Here's how you can (and probably do) get in trouble when you are NOT in your correct positions:

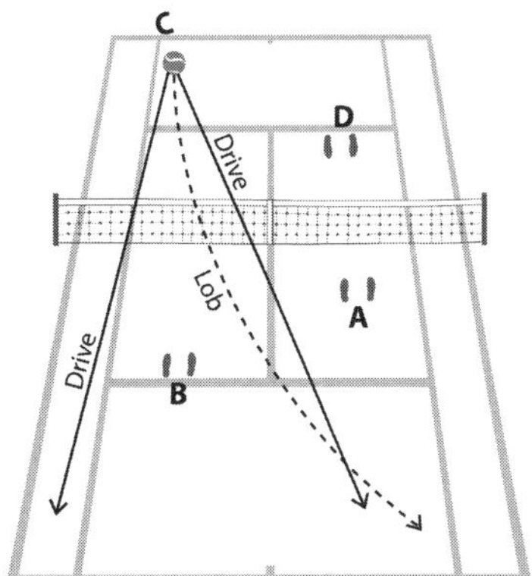

HELLE'S HINTS

Practice this without a ball.

You [A] and partner B are in your offense zone. Now imagine the ball is in C's court...and position yourself. Check it, talk to your partner, get used to where you each are, get familiar with the "sense" of position.

Now imagine the ball has shifted to D's court and move right away. Do this repeatedly and you will discover the diagonal lanes in which you'll always move.

You may want to begin this practice in slow-motion, calling out the shots and moves. Work up to game speed. This way, you can see how it takes time for you to move from one to the other. To change direction of the ball requires time (shot selection), so choose accordingly. Or your shot must be a put-away so it doesn't matter whether you have time or not.

13

LESSON THIRTEEN

breaktime: let's take a walk

Down the street from my home there is an open area and some small hills. When I walk in the morning, which I do often, with my black Lab, Homer. I walk up on these hills and just try to enjoy the beauty of Northern California, at least my part of it which lies just a few minutes north of the Golden Gate Bridge. Sometimes it is chilly and I can hear the fog horns on the bridge, but where I am, there is usually no fog and by early morning the sun breaks through the thin overcast and it is another of those magnificently beautiful days we are so used to. In Denmark, days like this came maybe ten times a year. Now, beautiful days are a nice habit.

On my return walk, I often play tennis in my mind—a tournament I was in a few days before, a match I watched on television, a game that took place a long time ago. A lesson where I discovered yet another way of explaining my system.

On one of these recent walks, it came to me that one of the strengths of Dynamite Doubles is its ability to let you play tennis Two Against One.

In the simplest of terms, here's what I mean. When I am returning a serve, I have to remember the FIRST and most important job I have to do and that's GET THE BALL BACK OVER THE NET. That's it, period. The essence of the game is to get the ball back over the net. Okay, I consciously think of that *every* time I am ready to return. Get the ball back over the net, Job One and avoid the net person, Job Two. But no fancy shot, no muscle, no show, just get-the-ball-back-over-the-net, period.

As soon as I hit the ball I know I have to hook up with my partner and gang up with her to protect our court against anything possible that our opponents might hit. One opponent hits, two of us are ready to defend. So here we are, *Two Players Against One.*

Think of the tiny little psychological things that just went on there. First of all, when I'm hitting the ball, there I was all alone—against two players across the net. That's not the kind of pressure you want against you when you're playing. As soon as I got the ball over the net, I connected with my partner and there were two of us and the emotional load was shared, dissipated and things weren't so bad anymore. Mind you, all this emotional ping-pong took place in just a couple of seconds.

My point in telling you this is that you should be aware of things like this are going on in your head. If you understand the process, you're on your way to being able to focus and concentrate better and this will improve your game in ways you never dreamed of. Keep it simple.

When I get the ball over the net and away from the net person, I have a better chance *with my partner* to protect against any shot back at us. And *both* of us have more time than if I hit to the closer opponent, their terminator.

I really *want* to play Two Against One whenever I can. If I have to play One (me) Against Two, I am putting pressure on myself and I can end up blowing the shot and risking the ire of my partner as well. Then *both* of us are in terrible emotional shape for the next point and, often we don't even know why. It's those little internal pressures that we're not aware of—such as the difference between Two-of-us-to-one-of-them versus the opposite.

What I want when I play doubles is for my opponents to play One Against Two, put the pressure on them, protect our territory, *practice patience,* and control the ebb and flow of the game. When the pressure, even this tiny, mostly unfelt pressure, is on them, I know my team will win a lot of free points.

Anyway, that's what happens when I take a walk. I like to exercise my body *and* my mind. Try it.

14

LESSON FOURTEEN

a review

DYNAMITE DOUBLES demands diagonal decisions. The workhorse must always be ready to take ① anything crosscourt, ② deep lobs and down the middle shots. The terminator shouldn't take a shot that is out of her reach over the middle OR intercept a crosscourt shot she can't turn into something offensive or positive.

If the workhorse keeps hitting crosscourt, the positioning remains unchanged—you don't have a lot of running around to do to defend 100% of your court. This is better than hitting shots where both you and your partner have to change positions *and* it's a lot more soothing to the emotional side of the game. It gives you a chance to look for an opening, find a weakness, build up a point, not to mention give your opponents a chance to make an error.

Your mind can constantly play ahead of your strokes. You breathe easier, physically and emotionally. The workhorse need not put the ball away.

Always try to be in the same major zone as your partner, defense zone or offense zone *when the ball bounces in your opponents' court.* You can be in separate zones when the ball is in your court, but immediately get together again as soon as you or your partner has hit the ball. Think about it, if you obey this simple rule, you're always in the same major zone and you're always positioned diagonally (staggered) to each other in relation to the ball in your opponents' court—therefore knowing who takes what shot or who is responsible for what shot. Both of you are facing the ball and the opponent who is going to hit it. She's playing One Against Two. No confusion on your side of the net, just smooth dancing.

This position ensures that you and your partner will always be in communication with one another *automatically* and it will forever end the confusion about whose shot it is. And, best of all for your bones, you'll never run into each other going for a ball again. Collisions are right now, as you read this, a thing of the past. The crosscourt workhorse will always be behind the terminator and take anything that escaped her—except, of course, for the down-the-line drive, which is never workhorse's responsibility, but always the terminator's.

It may be pursuing the obvious, but the roles and responsibilities of the workhorse are always evenly divided between partners because the server always assumes that role. Why? Because the serve has to go diagonally crosscourt*!* The returner of serve is also the workhorse since the ball is being hit diagonally across from her.

I always suggest to my students that the server hit the first volley crosscourt without too much angle. Why? It means you have to make the least adjustment while the server is getting herself into the offense zone and the two of you can start building up the point. It's hard enough to serve and run up to get in position for the first volley, so keep it simple and volley crosscourt, toward the crosscourt workhorse's feet—avoiding the net player on the other side. Once you are situated in the same zone as your partner, you can start working together to get your opponents out of position and find the opening you need to put away the winning shot.

ever wonder about this?

Up and back—how did this mystery begin? Ever wonder why we start doubles tennis games the way we do? Well, I'm going to try to explain it because if you understand this fundamental part of the game, you'll see how my system uses its wisdom. Actually, I tell this to most of my students about the second day of instruction.

The server is granted a "supposed" weapon, her serve, and this is "supposed" to be enhanced when she uses it, then comes up to the offense zone to meet with her partner. The returner is "supposed" to return crosscourt and come up to her offense zone to meet with *her* partner. At service, *the conventional formation is EXCELLENT*. In fact, it's what I've been telling you in this book so far, isn't it? Well, if it's so good, why do players give up this excellent formation as soon as the ball has been served?

Ask yourself that very slowly. Make yourself forget how you're playing now and how most of your friends play—understand that, at service, all four of you are in perfect position to play tennis. Now, if the server never comes to the net, what good is her partner doing there? If she did not get to intercept the return, she is now out of play and wasted.

Conversely, if the returner never comes up to the offense zone, why does her partner [D] start on the service line? If D did not move into her offense zone when partner C hit a crosscourt return, and intercept the shot from server A, she is now wasted. Most partners [D] become rooted there like a line judge. If she came to play tennis, standing on that line is the worst spot on the court to be after the return went crosscourt. So why does D start out on the service line? So she can be in the right place in case C's return goes straight to B. The wisdom and science of where players position themselves at service is wise and useful and we should remember why this great formula was given to every doubles player who ever walked on a court.

Be aware of how really good this positioning is, and you and your partner will never get confused or beaten down the middle. The conventional line-up, one-up, one-back, is designed for a reason: To make sure you cover 100% of the court and get together in the same major zone after the serve and return and keep the Diagonal Formula going: workhorse if the ball is crosscourt from you; terminator, if the ball is straight ahead on the same half of the court as you are.

You can see the benefits by knowing this:

"C" players win a lot by having one player up at the net and one back at the baseline. So do the young Juniors in the beginning.

"B" players have learned to come to the net, but now get caught a lot because they forget who was supposed to get which shot since they were both "at the net."

"A" and Open players develop *anticipation* and learn which shots they can make and which ones they can't. However, there is still a lot of confusion as to who closes in to kill and who covers the lobs.

Unless you use my system, I guarantee you the only doubles players who know which is really their ball to hit are the C players and the kids...because *"I am up, you are back. I kill at the net; you run everything down."* Okay, that's a winning strategy, but only at that level.

If you've gotten this far with me, you know it's a problem that's easy to fix. Take these same roles, but put the back player at the service line instead of at the baseline. She takes the same balls as before, but *volleys,* instead of letting the ball bounce. She has the same responsibilities, but she's now closer to her partner and much more dangerous to her opponents because she is hitting overheads and volleys and not giving her opponents the recovery time they need or like. Sure, she'll still have to chase the lob over her partner down and hit it after a bounce sometimes, but that gets easy to anticipate—and easy to avoid by changing the shot she hits prior to that.

Your other option is to put the "up" player back in the defense zone with the "back" player so you both are playing from the same major zone.

Does it work consistently? You bet it does. I have seen my students consistently win over players who were superior athletes and/or teams composed of upper-level singles players who "just didn't get it" when my Dynamites beat them. I've witnessed players who were disgusted or angry and about ready to give up the game, turn into marvelous, competitive doubles players. And I've watched newcomers to tennis gain confidence and enjoyment from learning Dynamite Doubles, the Diagonal Way.

Perhaps best of all, I've seen partners who had played together for a long time and were on the verge of ending both their tennis-playing and their friendship go on to winning, friendship-saving ways. For a coach and instructor who wants all of her players to do well, this method of playing doubles has been extremely worthwhile and fulfilling.

I also give the system total credit to my own success the past few years since I hardly ever take time to practice. I rely solely on my court positioning, shot selection and 100% faith in the Dynamite Doubles system, anticipation and the secure knowledge that if I can get to the ball, I can probably get it back over the net.

Let me take a moment here and once again urge you to do something—just two or three times—that you probably aren't doing now: Go watch some doubles. Watch for games where there are sparkling winning shots every once in a while and the team with the occasional and spectacular shots will probably be losing. Consistently. And watch for doubles games where two players blend together and become one. Notice how the flow of the point is smooth and the partners are always backing each other up. Watch for the "dancers"—couples who smoothly and effortlessly get into position to anticipate the next ball, and who sense where it is headed and know where to hit it.

After a while (and not very long at that), you'll begin to notice the most common problem in doubles today: Lack of patience and lack of trust between partners. You can see this when you start seeing poor shot selection and awkward mistakes and a lot of blame-making that takes place just below the surface.

"Mine!" or "Yours!" are the most-used, most problem-causing calls in doubles. The terminator can call "yours!" and *only* the terminator. The workhorse has to take all lobs that the terminator chooses not to take, so that call, "Yours!" from a workhorse is a complete and utter no-no. "Mine" isn't necessary unless the workhorse is helping the terminator remember to leave the lob for her. If the terminator wants the lob, she takes it—without saying anything and the workhorse takes anything else.

I recommend using "Mine!" only as an educational or informational call. The reason is simple. Talking and hitting simultaneously can be very distracting and if you've blasted out "*Mine!*" and then blow the shot, it is very hard to recover mentally. "*Yours!*" is the proper call and should come only from the terminator.

Visualize the zones on the court. Notice what happens when one team consistently returns the ball crosscourt and sets up a point with grace and style. Imagine yourself doing the same thing. See what happens when a team gets flustered and separated and doesn't divide the responsibilities. Watch the knives that are exchanged between partners when one or both of them make egregious errors. The sound you hear is not the ball-against-the-racquet. The sound you hear is a friendship breaking up. Or listen for the talkers, the ones who keep apologizing. For these players, tennis is becoming an exercise in apologia.

No more*!*

HELLE'S HINTS

Beauty or the Best? Your choice.

Quick quiz: What's best to learn? How to kill the ball and hit two or three great winners in an hour, or: how to play together with your partner, be in the right place at the right time and succeed as a Team? If you answered yes to the first part, you probably shouldn't be playing doubles and I bet you have trouble getting a partner. If you answered yes to the second part, you're sporting the right attitude and this book of Dynamite Doubles will help you enjoy your game for many years to come. Without doubt, you'll have more fun with your tennis game than you thought possible.

And you can be my partner any day.

15

LESSON FIFTEEN

the zone difference

If you've been playing doubles for more than a month, by now you can see that Dynamite Doubles is not far from the beginning doubles system that every player learns at the beginning of her recreational tennis career. By adding the zones, I have kept the same general rules in force, that is, one player retrieving and one player putting the ball away. However, when you practice what I preach, both players are in the same major zone so the gap between them is not so great and they're much more difficult to beat.

Now, the only difference is that your roles change every time the ball changes direction and players take turns so that it is not always the same one who hangs back nor the same one who puts the ball away.

Look, we all know that most points are won up at the net with volleys and overheads. However, there's always the fear of a lob that will get by you. You can see a lot of players who suffer from what I call "Lob Fear" starting to back up as the point is in play and consequently lose their position.

On the court, the most common thing I hear from my first-time students to my instruction to follow their shots up to the net is: "They're going to lob over us and I'll have to come back anyway, so why not stay back in the first place?" Well, there is only one answer to the lob and that's to hit it in the air with an overhead or high volley. So I tell them to come up to the net, but not too far—remember to slow down/pause when the ball bounces on the other side of the net, well before your opponent hits the ball. That way you can still react to a lob and hit it with an overhead or high volley, without letting it bounce.

If you stay back and let the lob bounce, your opponents are

under no pressure whatsoever. If you do come to the offense zone, you can challenge them over and over again to make a *perfect* shot and you are always keeping them under tremendous pressure.

Remember, in Dynamite Doubles, you spend most of the point in the offense zone and when someone says, "Come up to the net," that's a relative statement. Sometimes you may be in the top part of the offense zone as the terminator, and other times you may be on the back part at the service line, as the workhorse, anticipating a lob or covering for your partner. What you have to do, and this demands you pay attention to the type and style of tennis your opponents are playing, is to learn which shot to anticipate and get in position for that shot, whether it's a lob, a drive, or an angled short shot.

After hearing me for a few lessons repeating, "Serve and volley, Serve and volley*!*", one of my students started referring to this style of play as "Dancing Doubles" and calling her team the "Dynamites."

I can live with that.

When you "Diagonal Dynamites" are in the same zone and you're dividing the responsibilities between you, you have eliminated the biggest problem between doubles players. While you're both doing the "Diagonal Dance," you'll be gracefully dancing/playing the way the best doubles players in the world play instinctively. Doubles teams that seem to "click" on the court are usually not the great singles power hitters you see in finals matches on television. It is the players who know their positioning and shot selection via high-percentage placements who win in doubles. McEnroe and Martina are the exceptions and that is why they are so extremely exceptional. They have both. Consider McEnroe's 1996 comment on the Davis Cup Team selection: "I can suit up with my brother tomorrow and beat any team."

And I believe he can, because he is supremely skilled at four things:

1. shot selection.
2. positioning.
3. court coverage.
4. player responsibility.

These abilities are why he can make the claim. They provide him the confidence (not pure boast) to make such a statement. Look at the questions those four things solve: ❶ what, ❷ where, ❸ how, and ❹ who.

And McEnroe and Martina were consistent winners.

Watch a good professional doubles team and see how they dance together. Neither one ever gives up on their partner. A bad team often has one dancer and one spectator. It's not hard to spot if you watch doubles tennis to learn, not just as a spectator.

Let's say you've just made a

super shot and you need to re-position to cover 100% of the court with your partner. Most players often take that extra second to pat themselves on the back as they *watch their shot*—instead of moving, getting in position and thinking of what kind of shot is coming back at them. Hey, even some of the best-of-the-best super shots come back at you. You have to be ready, no matter what. Being ready means never being surprised that you have to hit a *follow* to your super shot.

So, here is a new way of thinking for you:

"There are no put-aways!"

"There are no winners!"

The ball is always coming back in your mind. It is just not all opponents who are able to get it back. Too bad, because you were ready. And you know what? Everyone will still remember the great shot you made that set up the winner. Some people call this win-win, I call it smart-smart.

16

LESSON SIXTEEN

refining the system

Help! Are we in offense? Are we in defense? How can we tell? Answering these two questions correctly is imperative if you are to choose the right shot at the right time, aiming it at the correct target and positioning yourself correctly on the court before and after the shot. Well, it's not as difficult as it seems.

EXAMPLE: You [A] and your partner B are both in the defense zone. Your opponents, C and D, are in their offense zone.

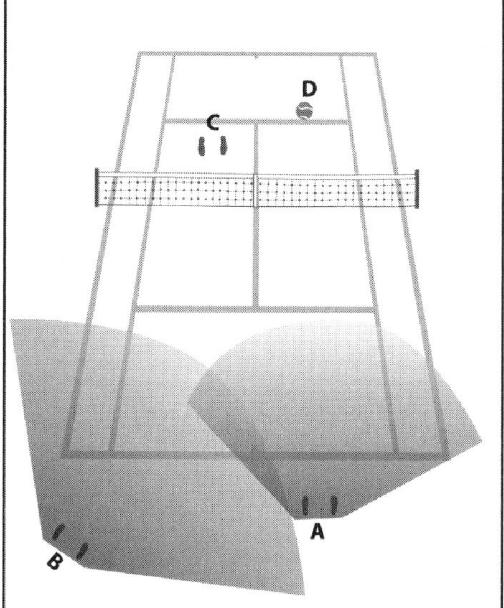

Look at the illustration. Try to imagine how much court you really have to cover here. You need legs and patience to play from the defense zone. The big deal here is that you're in the defense zone. That means your main goal is to vary your shots, mix up the pace, spins and the height of the ball to take control of the point.

How?

In defense, always let the ball bounce before you hit it. There's a good reason for this. You need time to hit and recover balls from here. Run balls down and mix up the pace, spin and height of your shots.

Give yourself room and make the best possible shot you can from here.

Lobs, down the line or above the middle, mixed with hard, flat drives down the line or crosscourt down the middle are the best shot selections from the defense zone. *But you must mix up your shots* so that your opponents in their offense zone will have to work harder for their shots. You don't have many angles to work with from the defense zone, so the height of your shot, and varying the pace are your best weapons from here. Topspin and slice shots are also good ways to mix it up.

If you get in the habit of only lobbing, your opponents can stand comfortably on or behind the service line and hit overhead smashes at you all day long. Mix in a hard drive or an occasional soft crosscourt low shot that brings your opponents forward again. Work at making them move forward and back, rather than side-to-side. When I'm in the defense zone, I try everything I can to keep my opponents from hitting down on the ball with an easy volley. They are trying to get every ball without a bounce and I am trying to make shots that they will have to let bounce, or I'll hit it so hard that they can barely get their racquet on the ball. I want them to hit defensively from their offensive zone and I want to hit offensive shots from my defense zone. This way I have equalized the situation, even though I am in my defense zone.

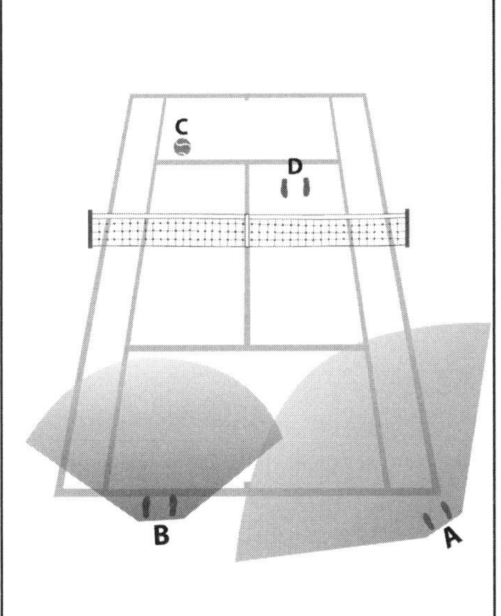

Mixing up your shots has a great reward, too—that look of utter surprise on the face and in the eyes of your opponents. If you want a nice rule to play doubles tennis by, here's one: Surprise Works.

Whatever your shot selection, make it a pattern that doesn't allow them to stand in one spot hitting the same shot over and over. Make them move*!* Get them to adjust to your shot and change the pace, work on *their* patience and consistency.

Recall, I don't expect to hit a winner from here, but I *am* looking for my opponents to make an error or weak volley that allows me to move into the transition zone, or offense zone, and hit an offensive passing shot. Now I've changed the pace of the game again and I'm keeping them off-balance.

the low angled dipper shot.

This is your lowest percentage shot from defense. If you hit a low, dipping crosscourt shot and your workhorse opponent has to hit up on the ball, you can expect something weak. You might get a high pop-up shot or a short-angled, dipping dropshot. In any case, you should be moving forward in anticipation of these shots as soon as you see your opponent is going to be taking the ball below the net.

Below the net shots limit them and you know you're not going to be in trouble as far as being killed with a smash and you can start to move forward anticipating a weak shot and, whooopee, a chance for you to take over the offense again. *But be careful!* If your soft, low shot is even a tiny bit off and sits up too high, you are dead because your opponents will close in and hit down and kill the ball. You should only try this shot when you think your opponents are expecting a lob, and you know you have a good chance of making it.

the drive.

If you hit a hard, flat drive from the defense zone straight at the net player down the line or crosscourt down the middle, you might get a hard, flat reflex volley right back at you or a mis-hit short dropshot. You must be ready to stay back and react f-a-s-t for the blocked reflex volley or sprint up (in case it's a short, mis-hit dropshot). Your drive can be great at the right time, but also can really mess you and your partner up if you're not alert. Volleyers love this shot anyway, so use it wisely. When your opponents expect a lob, for example, you surprise them with a drive right at them. Keep them off-balance by being unpredictable. If they have to wonder what you're going to hit, you have a definite advantage, you have control of the point.

Learn to add topspin to your drive so you can get the ball to spin downward toward their feet. This will make them hit up on the ball so you can maintain the control from defense.

the lob.

If you hit a high lob from defense which your opponents can return with an overhead, the ball will most likely come back toward you deep in the defense zone, *back up* before they hit it so you can have their shot in your "V" and be ready to retrieve the ball. Don't rush — you have until the second bounce to get to it so play your run accordingly. The crosscourt workhorse is farther back than her partner, who is closer to the ball. Both of you are facing the ball and reading the racquet in order to anticipate where the ball will come.

This way, even if it's a powerful shot that comes at you, at least you are way back behind the baseline, close to the fence in your defense zone expecting it and actually you have a very good chance of retrieving the ball. Do this a few times and the people on the other side of the net will start to wonder about what's happened to their "killer" strokes.

*In conclusion...*It's generally wiser to use the change-of-pace, change-of-height philosophy (lobs and drives) from defense. Wait until you get a shot that takes you into the transition zone before you really take advantage of the short, low crosscourt angle shot.

Singles players playing doubles hit these great ground strokes from defense, but don't mix them up enough with lobs and soft shots. This gives the opposing team an easy time in anticipating the hard, flat ground stroke. This is one of the reasons so many good singles players have trouble with the doubles game. The strategy difference between the two games is immense.

the key lob.

Lobs are the key shots from the defense zone. Against right-handers, lob from the deuce court—mostly to get the ball over both of their backhand shoulders. Lob either down the line over their terminator or over the middle crosscourt—but not too wide.

From the ad court you can't get to the backhand shoulder of the crosscourt opponent; it will go out. Stick with down the line, over the terminator and over the middle crosscourt.

Your lobs don't have to be unreachable for your opponents—just good enough so they can barely get to them and have to take a little off their overhead in order to make them. Height is more important than depth on your defensive lobs, so practice hitting real sky-high lobs to buy time. Make your lobs so your opponents have to hit from behind the service line in order to make the shot. If you telegraph your lobs and your opponents can read them well in advance, you have absolutely no chance of surprising them and both of them will have stepped back in anticipation and have a good chance to hit a powerful smash. If you attempt to hit the perfect lob that hits the back of the line for a clear winner...don't bother; it won't work.

Besides, what's happened to your patience? Did you forget how difficult it is to make an outright winner from the defense zone? It is always much wiser to tire out your opponents, both mentally and physically, by making them reach up high for overheads and way down low for the low volleys or half-volleys. You want to be in charge and it's always a good idea to let them self-destruct and ruin their own game by running out of patience and trying to hit a lot of winners with low-percentage shots. Remember, you are in your defense zone.

keep watching.

If you will do as I suggest and go out every once in a while and just watch a little doubles play, you'll see that time after time pretty good players will be trying to hit their way through their opponents from the defense zone and rushing up after their shot—only to be nailed right at their feet in the transition zone.

If you want to drill a shot from the defense zone, you must wait and see what your opponent does with the shot. Remember, you must pause and get ready to split-step when your ball clears the net which is pretty soon after you drilled your shot. Most likely, the only thing she can do is block it and the ball will either fly out or come right back to you, bouncing in the transition zone or deeper. *Then* if you stay back, you can hit another one...or choose a lob to mix up the pace for a surprise. Always keep in mind, one of the most fundamental rules of the game of tennis: The harder you hit the ball, the less time you have to react to the next shot.

You'll be a better doubles player if you play smart from the defense zone and think in terms of forcing a mistake from your opponents, rather than trying to make a grandstand winning shot. Let the other guys hit lots of shots. Most (or much) of the time, they'll try to go for a winner because they're in offense and think they ought to win the point outright, now, if not sooner.

What will start to drive them crazy after a while is the fact that you and your partner are not where they are used to seeing players across the net. Their targets have moved and now instead of hitting your feet at the service line, they are trying to find you on the baseline or deeper and their shots are going out. They have lost their target and their focus. You're doing something right and they can't quite figure it out. Frustration will build up and they will have given away the mental part of the game and you *know*, you really *know* who's going to win today.

The team on offense likes to think it sets the pace of the game, but there is no reason in the world for you to accept this fact. You want to be dictating to them, not the other way around. That's why you constantly mix up your shots. If you get in real trouble, put up a skyscraper—a really high defensive lob and buy some time for you and your partner to adjust and read the overhead.

lob "looks"

By the way, when you lob, D-O-N-'-T look up in the air and stare at the ball all the way. First, hit your lob by really watching the ball and following through, making sure it gets up there, *then* watch the person who's going to hit it.

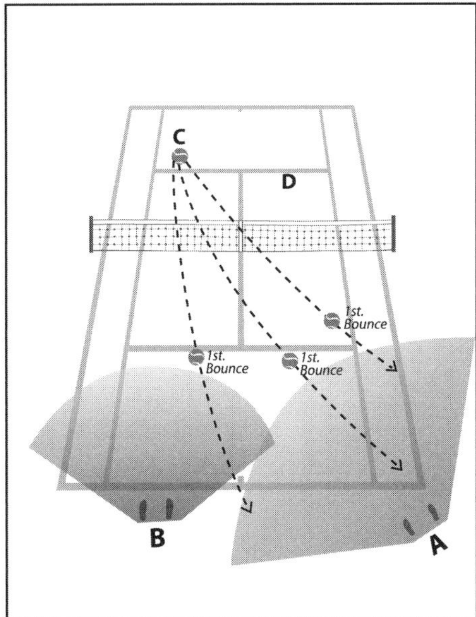

Read her feet, body and racquet. Is she going to hit an overhead smash? Is she letting it bounce? Is she hitting a backhand? If she is hitting an overhead smash on the fly, you and your partner must quickly scoot backwards to position yourselves in the Up-and-Back Position in your defense zone with the crosscourt player behind her partner, facing the ball and the person who's going to hit it.

The forward player is closer to the baseline, and the center mark, facing the ball and the opponent straight ahead, ready for a shorter overhead, ready to run forward and scramble on a mis-hit ball.

See what's happened here? You and your partner have divided up the defense zone just as you did the offense zone, using the same formula. The crosscourt player is the workhorse and the closer player is the forward player. There is another reason not to watch your own lob all the way. What if they misjudge the shot and can't hit it on the fly? Then you have to react to that. Also, if the sun is out, you don't have to look up into the sun while tracking the ball.

Finally, if they choose to hit your lob with a backhand overhead, you know it won't be as powerful as a forehand overhead. It will more likely be an angled shot and it will be a lot weaker and shorter than the forehand overhead smash, so you can anticipate that and start to move *diagonally* forward, a little bit in anticipation. Your opponent's body language will tell you how good your lob was.

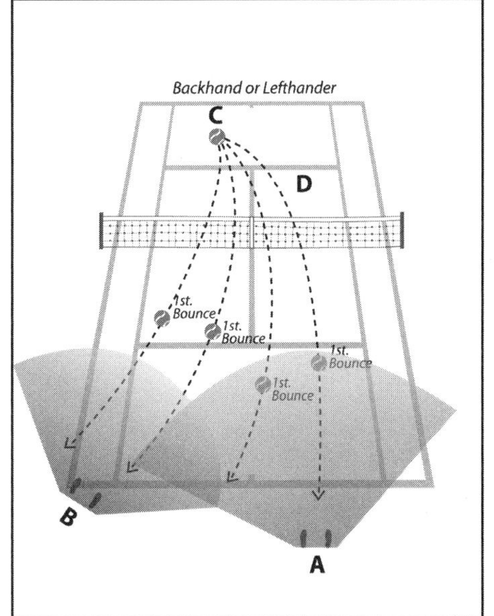

why the system?

~ a personal view ~

Now that you're beginning to see my system at work and have some understanding of how it will really improve your doubles game, let me tell you the why of Dynamite Doubles.

This style of play, with its emphasis on strategy and tactics, is designed so players can team up and hook up as dance partners, without ever having played together previously. They know instinctively who takes which shot, where to position themselves and what shot to hit in order to maintain team harmony. At my club, we presently have 8-10 full women's tennis teams in various leagues and it really helps to have a system to follow. If one player is unavailable, it's easy to make a replacement...if the system is used.

Also, I got very tired (and so will you) of hearing the common complaints or concerns: Does she have a strong forehand or backhand? Does she come to the net? Does she stay back? With the system you can play together whether she "stays back" or "comes in." We have the zones and we know how to play the zones together. This is a very unselfish system where you play with your partner in the major zones and that's the only thing that matters. You develop a wonderful, unselfish attitude that helps your game more than you can imagine.

The system allows you to give of yourself, be patient and tolerant and to work with your partner in a special and meaningful way. It's good for your head and it's good for your game. What a deal*!*

The only question I hear now from the women at my club is, "Does she play the system?" Now that's all that matters and fortunately, most of our players at the club do play the system today.

HELLE'S HINTS

Your opponents give you an awful lot of information in how they prepare for a shot. Watch them get ready to hit the ball and you'll have the ball in your sight and be ready to Read and React to their shot as they're hitting it.

Ask yourself, "What kind of shot is she going to hit?"

Is it a forehand?

Is it a backhand?

Is it a volley?

Is it an overhead?

Is her racquet above the net?

Is her racquet below the net?

Is she ready, well-balanced?

Is she in trouble, off-balance?

Is she going forward?

Is she going backward?

How would I hit that same shot in the same situation?

Practice again with two players in the offense zone and two players in the defense zone. The goal of this drill is to stay in your designated zone until the point is over and to work on your positioning and patience.

A player from the defense zone team may have to run forward to get to a ball, but must try to retreat back to defense and continue from there.

A player from the offense zone team may have to go to transition or defense zones to get a ball, but must immediately move up to the offense zone again.

Play first team to reach ten points and then…switch roles. This is a dynamite drill for Dynamite Doubles.

The offense zone team plays "No Bounce" to stay aggressive and speed up the game, and the defense zone team plays close to the "second bounce" to slow down the game.

17

LESSON SEVENTEEN

the anticipation chapter

I've been writing so much about anticipating shots and I know that's a part of the game that most mystifies some of my students. Here's a quick reminder of the Rules of Anticipation—things to watch for that allow you to anticipate shots from your opponents so that you can be there, ready and waiting, when the ball arrives.

The result should be that you'll be able to "tune in" to the game and be able to better seize the opportunities which lie before you on the court *as the ball is coming toward you.*

For example, in the defense zone, after a lob (don't watch the ball all the way to its peak!), you see your opponent standing right underneath where it will land and she looks so ready you wish you were doing the wash instead of playing tennis. Instead of standing and watching, get moving with your partner waaay back in the defense zone and anticipate a quite hard smash from her. Remember, workhorse covers the extreme angle and deep shots and the forward player is ready to take any short shot or a straight ball. You must anticipate where the *second* bounce will be and get to that spot before the ball does. Give yourself as much time as possible to get to the ball.

On the other hand, if your opponent is scrambling backwards and can barely get her racquet on the ball, her shot is likely to be shallow and weak and therefore you ought to be ready—don't move yet—to move forward (into the transition zone) in order to nail the next shot right down the middle or at her feet as a passing shot—also to give your opponents as little time to recover as possible. You learn to anticipate by watching your opponents' position in relation to the ball. Notice how they're preparing for the shot, react accordingly. It's amazing, but sometimes a not-so-good shot (in your opinion) could turn out to be a terrific shot because it totally surprised the people on the other side of the net and they were not ready to hit it.

It's that kind of game. And when you learn to anticipate, you have taken yourself to a new level and your scores and your partner will start telling you so.

Remember what I said waaay back in the beginning about the "V"? You should always face in the direction of where the ball is coming from, so you should find yourself pivoting with little shuffle steps or little split-steps so you can face the oncoming ball and feel it is coming right into your "V"—your belly button, your Sphere of Influence. You face differently depending on whether your opponent is hitting a forehand or a backhand. Learn (observe and remember) how natural her follow-through is from each position.

This position makes you think diagonally and changes the dimensions of the court. This position makes you think diagonally and changes the dimensions of the court. Yes, I said that twice. Think about it.

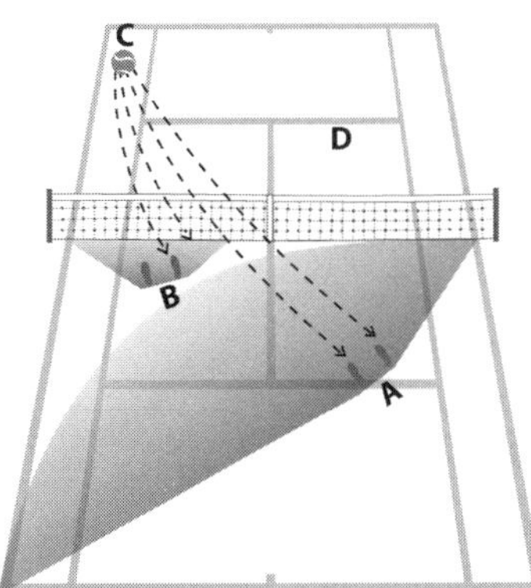

"turning the court".

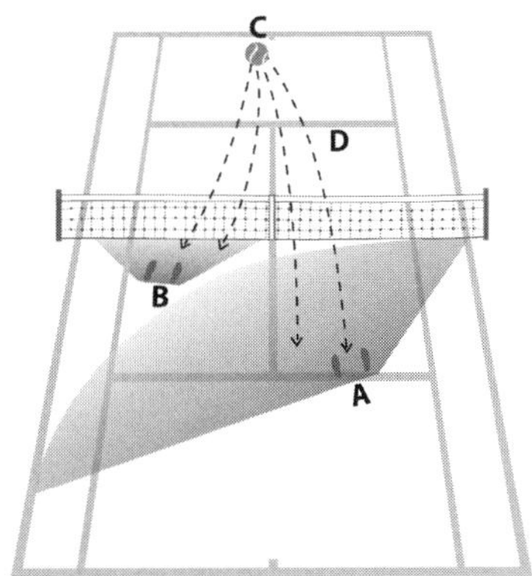

Notice the terminator turns slightly. The workhorse turns the court 45 degrees when the ball is wide and on the outside of her crosscourt opponent.

The "V" allows you to "turn the court" and to be in a ready position so you can defend against any shot, prepare for and hit the ball back to where it came from without changing direction.

As you move, the "V" changes. In order to get behind the ball, you must have the ball in front of you, in your "V."

If you get used to "seeing the 'V'" from every place on the court, you will always have the court you are responsible to cover within your "V" and it will be far easier to anticipate shots than ever before.

18

LESSON EIGHTEEN

where do I serve, coach?

If you serve up the middle, you decrease the angle at which your opponent can return the ball. This gives your partner a chance of poaching (cutting off the ball) and puts you in a better position for your second shot. That is by far the best percentage serve, however I have found that serving to the backhand is very effective and more predictable as far as what kind of return I get. My partner seems more likely to get involved and the backhand is often the opponent's weaker side. In the deuce court when I serve down the middle T, I get the backhand and the no angle return, so there I get two for one and win lots of easy points that way. I serve about 85% down the middle on the deuce court for that exact reason. Every now and then I will go wide or AT the opponent to mix it up and check their return and will let my partner know in advance, so she can be ready for the possible down the line shot. In the ad court, I generally serve about 60% wide to her backhand and the rest up the middle T with an occasional serve AT my opponent. When I serve at my opponent, I aim for her left hip in order to attempt to jam her.

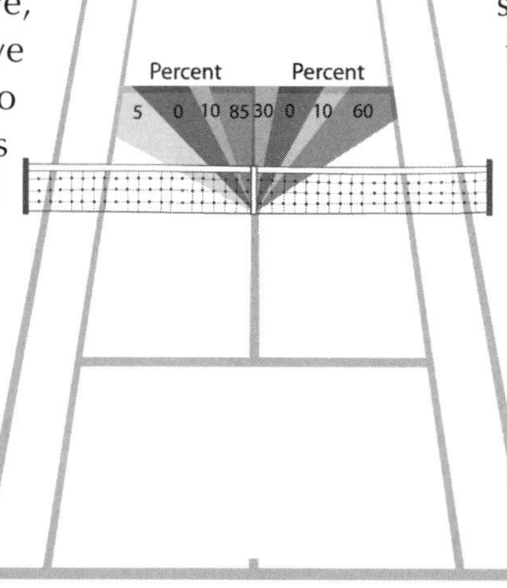

Also, disguise your aim when you serve. I do the same routine whether I serve wide or down the middle. I wait until contact with the ball to direct the ball with my racquet head and wrist snap where I want it to go. That way opponents can't anticipate and get a jump start on me.

where should I stand, coach?

The best place to serve from is about halfway between the doubles line and the center mark. From here, you're closer to your "home" split-step mark (see "Definitions") in the offense zone and you don't give your opponent too much of an angle to work with on the return. You always want to run forward in a slight diagonal line following your ball after you serve. You are also ready for a down the middle return, and a lob over your partner which are the most-likely shots to come if you serve down the middle T.

If you stand too wide, close to the "home" in the defense zone by the singles sideline when serving, you give your opponents too much angle to work with and your partner at the net has a tough time covering anything at all, never being able to cut anything off and you are in for a long and lonely service game. Players who serve and stay back in the defense zone do this a lot, and find it difficult ever getting to the offense zone with their partner, and wonder why they are having to work so hard, never getting any help from their partner. So where you stand when serving can make a huge difference in how your partnership works, how the point plays out and whether you win your serve or not.

If server A stays back in the defense zone after her serve, she should still serve from the spot mentioned above (half way between the doubles side line and the center mark) and then immediately move a couple of shuffle steps to the right in the deuce court and to the left in the ad court to "get back Home," face the ball and be ready for the return. So you see no matter what, you have to move after your serve whether you stay back in the defense zone or are coming into transition towards the offense zone.

return of serve.

In this example, returner C has to get the ball over the net just to get a chance of winning the point. The sad fact is that too many returns are missed—mostly by hitting the ball into the net. My philosophy here is simple: Always give your opponents a chance to miss*!*

Especially on a return of serve.

From a server's standpoint, remember how difficult that first volley is? Your job as a returner is to get the ball in play and let that difficulty help *you.*

As a workhorse, there are two definite split-step marks, "homes" you must recognize and get as close to as you can after each shot. The same thing applies to the terminator—two "homes" you must try to recover to after each shot.

One is in offense and one is in defense. terminator, your split-step marks are diagonally in front of the workhorse's, and you are closest to the ball. Look at these illustrations. Can you tell where the ball is?

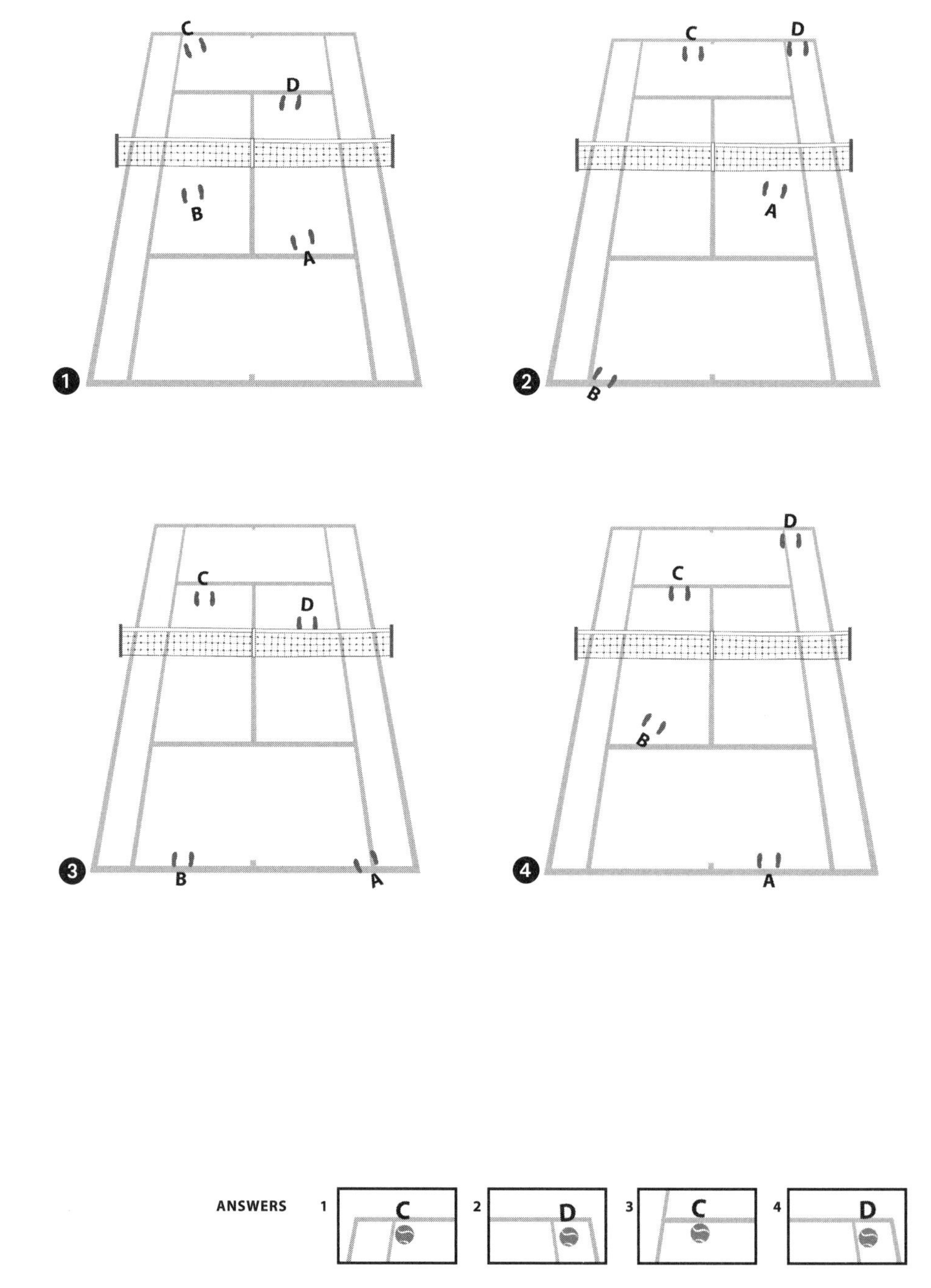

where should I stand to receive serve?

If you're right-handed and you're up against a right-handed server in the deuce court. I start out close

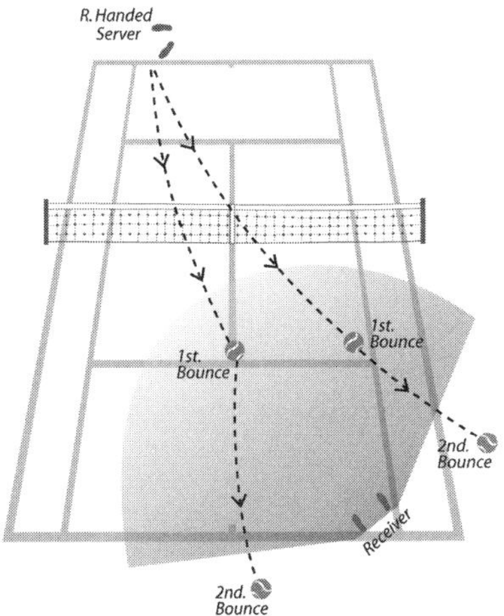

to my split-step mark in the defense zone and face the server and the oncoming ball, right foot on the singles line, left foot on the baseline. You can adjust this (slightly) depending on where your opponent serves from and how she serves. Remember the "V" stance. You can move sideways, forward or go back,

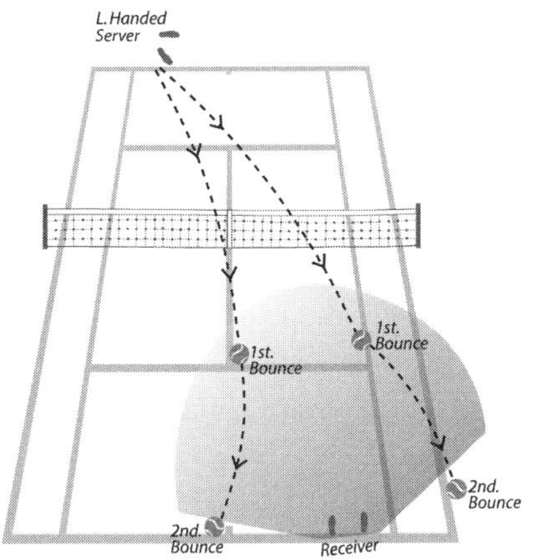

keeping the same "V." The server and the service box corners must be in your "V."

If she serves from her alley, you will have to move diagonally forward, and out toward the alley, into the transition zone and pivot more, to cut off the angle she has created so you can see the server, the ball, and both corners of your ser-

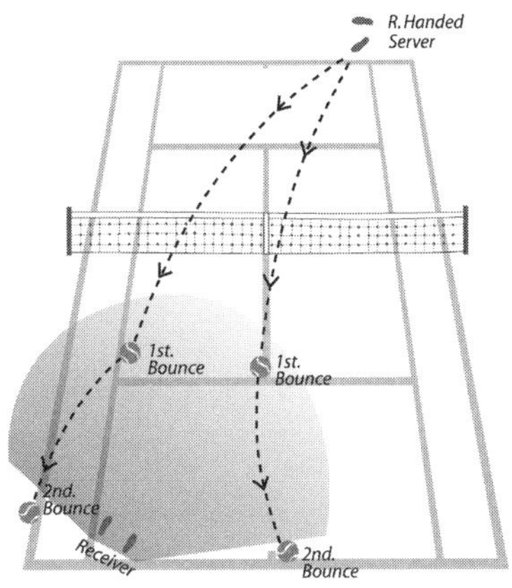

vice box within your "V" funnel.

If she serves more from the center of the court, you should move more to the center as well since the angle is decreased and a straight serve to your T is more likely.

If you're receiving serve, draw an imaginary line from the server to one corner of the service box and another to the other corner of the box. If the serve is going to be "in" it must come between these two (imaginary) boundaries. Position yourself in the middle of those two lines and you have the best possible coverage.

After a few serves, you can adjust to the server's pattern, but start out in the middle, adjust from there.

the evil lefties.

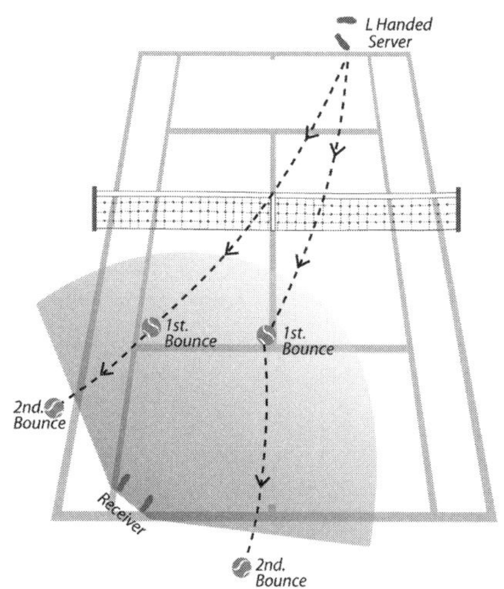

They can get to our body or backhand every time they serve, it seems.

Against a left-hander, you will get more serves down the middle in the deuce court and out wide in the ad court. Therefore, move toward the center, along the baseline in the deuce court and stand more toward the alley, turning and facing the server in the ad court.

Right handed or left handed, NOW you are finally ready to receive the serve. Where are you going to return the ball, what's your target? Over the net. Here's a suggestion that's more of a rule: STAY AWAY FROM THE NET PLAYER. You're playing doubles and you don't have to finish the point all by yourself. Besides, there are three perfectly good targets at which you can aim.

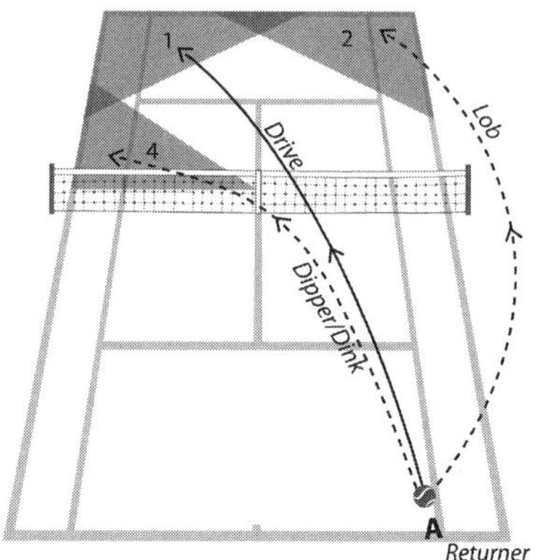

TARGET #1: Crosscourt, back toward the server, aiming at her feet, if possible, not changing direction of the ball.

TARGET #2: Lob in a straight line over net person's outside shoulder, thereby changing direction of the ball.

TARGET #3: Short angle crosscourt aiming in front of the corner of the service line and the sideline.

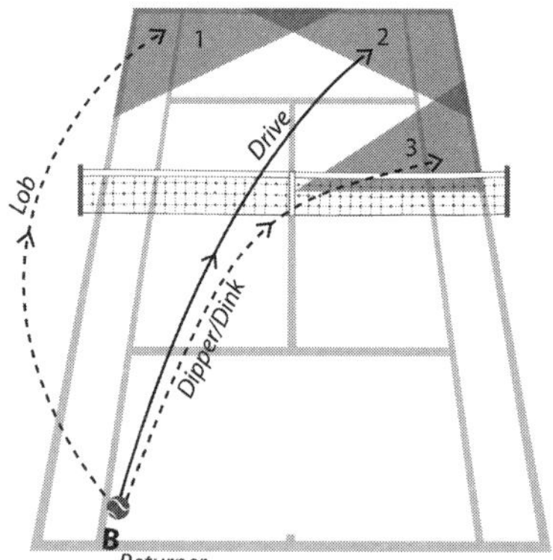

Hint: This is easier if you have moved into the transition zone to return.

Helle's first rule of Doubles is "Get the ball over the net," and Helle's second rule of Doubles is "Stay away from the net person."

Therefore, if you are having trouble avoiding the net person when returning serve, try to stay farther back to buy more time to get set for your return, so you can get the ball past the net player with either a drive or a lob. This little change in timing may just be enough to baffle your opponents for a moment and then cause an error from them. You have regained some confidence in your return of serve and given your opponents something extra to think about.

As a returner, you can stand anywhere to return, so the fences are the limits. Stay in the middle of those imaginary lines you've drawn in your "V" so you have an equal amount of court to cover, right and left. You may also choose to move forward into the transition zone (especially when someone serves with a sharp angle) and merely try to block the ball back without much backswing of the racquet. In baseball terms, this is similar to a bunt and can be very effective *if you IMMEDIATELY move* OUT of the transition zone after your return.

Okay, I return. Then what?

It depends on how difficult the serve was, where you returned it to, and where you ended up after returning it.

Your primary goal is to get into the *offense* zone with your partner and put pressure on your opponents. But if the serve was so good that all you did was get the ball back, you may benefit from recovering to your "home" in the defense zone, and with a few lobs get your partner back there with you or with a soft dink make the opponent hit up to you with a weak short shot which allows you to come up to the offense zone with your partner.

Be sure to recover to one of your "home" split-step marks on the court after your return. Now ask yourself where you should move after you've made these returns of serve **from the transition zone**. (Both feet in transition zone when hitting the ball.)

Crosscourt toward the server.
Move to the service line and split-step, facing the ball. You are at the workhorse "home" in offense zone.

Short crosscourt angle.
Move to workhorse "home" in offense zone, facing the ball.

Lob over net person.
Move to terminator "home" in offense zone, facing the ball.

Drive at net person.

Stay where you are, split step and face the ball. Be ready to read and react. You have no time to move after your hit, however be ready to chase down whatever shot comes back from the net player. Remember to split-step/hop as your opponent hits the ball.

Now let's say you're returning **from the defense zone**. (Both feet in defense zone when hitting the ball.)

❶

Crosscourt toward the server.
Stay in workhorse "home" in defense zone, facing the ball.

❷

Short crosscourt angle.
Stay in workhorse "home" in defense zone, facing the ball.

❸

Lob over net person.
Move forward to terminator "home" in offense zone, facing the ball.

Drive at net person.
Stay in terminator "home" in defense zone, facing the ball.

Other Decisions. If you're playing against a serve-and-volleyer, you have to make a decision right away as the receiver. ① Should I come to the net as well? ② Should I stay back in the defense zone? ③ Should I take up golf?

Well, whatever you decide from options ①, ② and ③, then by all means DO IT*!* And do it right away. Most players end up thinking about their options and doing nothing. What happens, class? Many voices: "YOU GET CAUGHT IN NO-(WO)MAN'S LAND*!*" And where's that, class? Many voices: "THE TRANSITION ZONE." Right you are. You may take the rest of the day off.

Wait*!* Not you. Stay with me here. If you decide to follow your crosscourt return in toward the offense zone against a serve-and-volleyer, the most important thing to remember is that you're in a footrace to see who gets there first. Consequently, you should take the return as early as possible which means *on the rise* and from the *transition zone*. On the rise means before the peak of the bounce, and you have to physically be moving toward the ball as you hit it and be in the transition zone when you contact the ball. You can chip the return or come over the ball, but in either case, take hardly any backswing as you move toward the ball and meet it early, in front of you, on the rise, before the peak.

Balance and timing are very important and your footwork and prep-time are also key factors to a good return. You don't need a big backswing because you're using the speed of the oncoming ball and you are on the move. Simply turn and let the face of your racquet meet the ball out in front. Transition your weight forward as you meet the ball on the rise. *Be sure to follow through with a firm wrist.* The ball comes off your racquet very fast and gives the server less time to react to your return. You may win the footrace to the offense zone now and catch the server with the ball at her feet. I compare this return from the transition zone to a bunt in baseball. Baseball players bunt and *quickly* must make it to first base. By the same token, you should move as fast as you can to your offense zone "home" and split-step to the opponent's hit.

If you play (or watch) a lot of doubles, you'll see good doubles players use this shot much more frequently than singles players who will use a regular big backswing ground stroke for a return and be planted in defense zone as they swing. This means they'll be recovering in their defense zone as well. Or, if they attempt to come forward after completing the return, they invariably get caught in their transition zone. The whole idea here is to find ways to "get to the net," that is get to your offense zone "home" (or as close to it as possible), faster than your opponent, and split-step to her hit. The rules say the server has to start from behind the baseline, so you can get a good jump on her by moving in and hitting the return sooner from your transition zone.

What if the server doesn't come to the net following her serve?

First, you know you are coming to the net. You are under less pressure, so you can focus on hitting one of your three options: deep crosscourt, short angle, or down the line lob. You want to take advantage of the opponents being in different zones by getting to the same major zone, offense in this case, with your partner and play Two Against One. I like the crosscourt options the best myself. This way I just come to the offense zone workhorse "home" split-step mark and wait and see what happens. You have your partner in front of you. She closes in and puts pressure on the opponent. You take the lob and the crosscourt shots. The server wishes she had taken up golf and her partner does, too*!*

If you lob the return over the net person, you have changed the direction of the ball and are now the terminator. You must try to get to your next "home" position—*as the terminator in the offense zone,* and your partner is now the workhorse in the offense zone. The lob is most effective as a surprise shot against a serve and volleyer.

It is more difficult than when you return crosscourt. The key here is to understand and remember that when you change the direction of the ball, you and your partner must change roles. New role = New Positions, New Responsibilities.

When I teach the Juniors at my club, I ask them to call out what role they are in after each shot. Two twelve-year olds challenged their fathers who came to me afterwards and asked, "What's this 'terminator!' stuff you've been teaching our sons? Every time the ball went over the net we heard one of them yelling, 'terminator, terminator!' and we couldn't figure out what they were doing."

The two Juniors were taking turns poaching—closing in, terminating and X-ing out the point. They were having so much fun confusing their dads and playing Dynamite Doubles at the same time, they never went for the same ball and they always knew who should take the lob and who should poach. Now the dads are on my court learning *how* to terminate, *when* to terminate, and *where* to terminate. Hey, folks, this works.

REMINDER: When you get to the court and warm up and first begin to play, you should begin to take inventory of your opponents. Watch to see what kind of game they intend to play. Most players have only one style of play and they pursue it relentlessly, win or lose. You can take advantage of this by studying their habits and adjusting your game. If a player doesn't ask for any overheads (or only one or two), you can assume she's not comfortable at the net and doesn't plan on hitting (m)any. Now you know to bring her to the net and make her hit volleys and overheads. If a player seems uncomfortable or timid about the ball at the net, take note of it and plan on driving some balls towards her as well as lobbing her. If one player starts at the net and hits great volleys and overheads, you need a strategy to keep the ball away from her at the net by lobbing, hitting wide crosscourt, changing pace and taking the net before she does. You will also have to hit right at her to keep her honest and show you are not intimidated by her. You and your partner may decide to start out very aggressive and take the offense and see who prevails. Remember, your team plays equally well from defense as from offense and you can switch back and forth any time. (If you can't, go out and practice that.)

As you can see, Dynamite Doubles puts you in command of the game, no matter what type of opponents you are playing. You are a team and you work together and you're always on the same page *every time your opponents hit a ball.* In order to play your position fully, use the full armory of your shots.

Always know where your opponents are and know whether they're in defense, offense or SPLIT. If they're in defense, you better be in offense with your partner. Conversely if they're in offense, you have two options: offense or defense. If they're split, you can be in *either* offense or defense, but be together. Do not be split. When your mother told you "two wrongs don't make a right," she was talking about the game of Dynamite Doubles.

When all four players are in the offense zone—hold your ground! Don't back up! Keep your racquets out in front and block the ball with reflex volleys. The point will be over very quickly. Stay with it and think: Close in! Terminate! Don't change direction!

The big problem I see in club tennis is (you guessed it) the lack of patience. If you're forced back in the defense zone, you are usually so eager to get back to offense that you forget you must get there in steps. Most of you survive the difficult shots and as soon as you get a chance to hit a strong drive or lob, you rush to the net regardless of where your opponents are.

Now, you get caught in the transition zone and the point is over.

The three most important rules of doubles, in case you've missed them up to this point are: 1, Patience. 2, Patience. 3, Patience.

HELLE'S HINTS

Look, it takes time, footwork and thinking to get out of the defense zone. When you can stay calm when you're pushed back into defense and not panic, you've mastered a whole new concept of doubles and taken your game up a level—maybe more. As a result, your offense play will blossom. And when I say yours, I mean your Team.

Most teams are only comfortable in one of the two major zones, so practice again and again until you feel at home in both.

The best doubles teams play all the zones and each partner knows what to do in each zone. They always recover in the same major zone and they mutually understand that you can be in all zones several times during a point.

Again, you can be in all zones several times during a point. Also remember, you can hit offensive shots from the defense zone and defensive shots from the offense zone. Dynamite Doubles is a flexible system of play that allows you to improvise and be creative on the court.

Know that and chances are you know more than those two people across the net from you. If knowledge is power, then you now have the power.

Here it is, Helle's handy-dandy **seven-pointed star**, the basic rules you can take to the court and play winning doubles—today.

1

Always face where the ball is coming from and let the ball come into your "V".

2

Know your "home" positions on the court—2 in offense zone, 2 in defense zone, depending on whether you are the workhorse or the terminator.

3

Know your responsibilities as a terminator and as a workhorse.

4

Recover to a major zone AFTER your hit and BEFORE your opponent's hit.

5

READY, READ and REACT*!*

When the ball you hit bounces in your opponents' court, get Ready to split-step as your opponent's racquet moves to strike the ball, so you can Read what is coming and React to the oncoming ball.

6

A point is never over until the ball bounces the second time. Never give up. There are no put-aways! HANG IN THERE. The ball is always coming back*!*

7

Doubles is a game of angles and percentages. And Patience.

LOOK FOR A COPY IN THE BACK OF THE BOOK AND STICK IT ON YOUR FRIDGE.

19

LESSON NINETEEN

triangles & diamonds "are a girl's best friend"

There is a theory of life, of sports, of writing, that says something to the effect, "Save the best for last." Now that you know how to play as a team, what your overall responsibilities and roles are, I want to admit to you openly and above board, that Dynamite Doubles The Diagonal Way works better with some shots than others. You knew that.

Which brings me to Triangles and Diamonds.

When I play doubles, four triangles pop out in my mind constantly, and I visualize them on the other side of the net. They're 1, 2, 3, and 4 above.

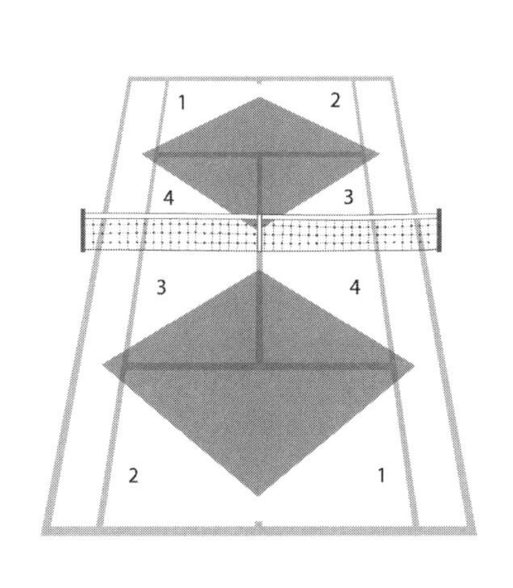

I always have three triangles (which ones, you'll see in a moment) that are available to me and I know I can get out of trouble when I succeed in hitting one of these targets (which one, I'll tell you in a moment). Better than that, I *know* I can turn a troubled situation into good offense and possible an instant winner doing this. So here and now, I'm sharing with you Helle's Secret of the Triangles.

And I *am* being serious here, I just want to present this to you in a comfortable way. If we were on the court at my club right now, what I'd probably do is play crosscourt from the defense, and every time the ball lands in triangle #1 call out, "YES!" When the ball lands short, call out "NO!" The usual pattern for this exercise sounds like: Yes-No-Yes-No-Yes-No-Yes-No, etc. This lets you know that when you hit into a triangle, you very often get a non-triangle shot back at you. Exactly what you want!

But we're not on the court, so I direct your attention to the illustration again and ask you to note that there are four triangles, 1, 2, 3, and 4. The hypotenuse of each triangle (that's the longest side) forms one side of a large diamond. This sounds complicated on paper, but just look at the illustration and it's very clear and simple. This diamond can be one of your most important targets at times.

Knowing where the triangles are in relation to your upcoming shot is very important to winning doubles and I bet you're dying to ask me why.

Simple.

If you can place your shot in one of your opponent's triangles at any given time from any place on the court, you can not only get yourself out of a lot of trouble during a point, but you can also turn bad situations into great opportunities. You'll play good, *solid* doubles this way and build up the point and eventually open up your opponent's court for the down-the-middle winner. The triangles are the hardest to defend against. That's why I try so hard to hit them.

This is very important. The three triangles are targets used to avoid the terminator on the other side of the net. If you can make *their* workhorse hit all the balls, you will create confusion, frustration and tap your opponents' patience. The result: they'll make errors and wrong shot selections. Make your opponents' workhorse do all the work by moving the ball around her terminator. You've learned to play with patience, and she probably hasn't. You will usually win.

On our side of the net, our terminator knows which shots are hers and our workhorse knows as well. This spells coordinated teamwork and it means winning doubles.

Here's the **RULE OF THE TRIANGLES**: Your opponent has hit one of the triangles on *your* side of the court, you have to avoid the opponent's terminator who is feeling and tasting the opportunity to win the point, and aim back at a triangle instead. If you make this shot, you'll neutralize the potential trouble you were in—or better, reverse the trouble to the other side of the net, so that *you* can begin to taste and smell a chance of winning the point. You have done your job, which is to avoid *their* terminator. If their workhorse gets it, you are challenging her to avoid your terminator, which probably isn't her game plan. Right? Right. Right on!

I know, I know, it seems difficult when you look at it on paper to hit those Triangle Targets, but, remember, you have some incredible angles to work with from your side, Let me show you.

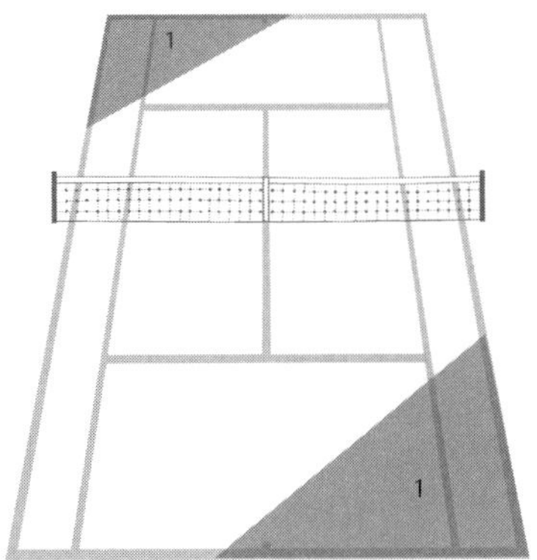

Put yourself and your partner in these illustrations. Oh, do it in your mind and pretend you're Center Court, Wimbledon. The main thing to look at is the shots you going to make—also in your imagination. Think of this: Deep Triangles to Deep Triangles, Short Triangles to

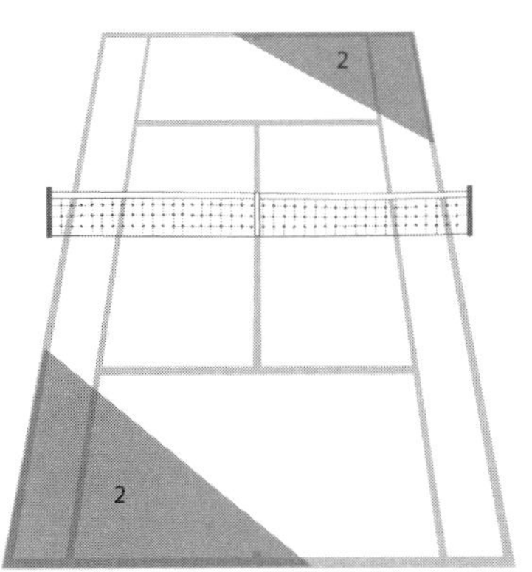

Short Triangles. Go ahead, hit a few balls in your imaginary Center Court, be my guest That wasn't so hard, was it? Most of all, do you see what was happening when you did that. Couldn't you feel your opponents going after the shots, yourself getting into position and

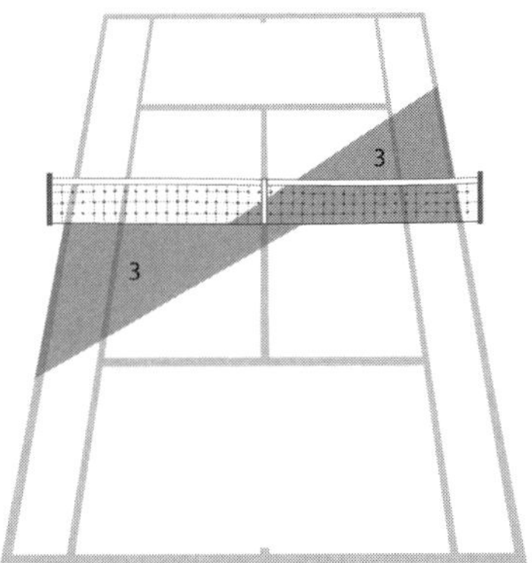

being ready to Terminate or take advantage of the situation as soon as your opponents don't answer with a triangle shot?

You (loud voice): "Yes*!*"

If you watch the points in a doubles match (as a spectator), you will see that most often a return

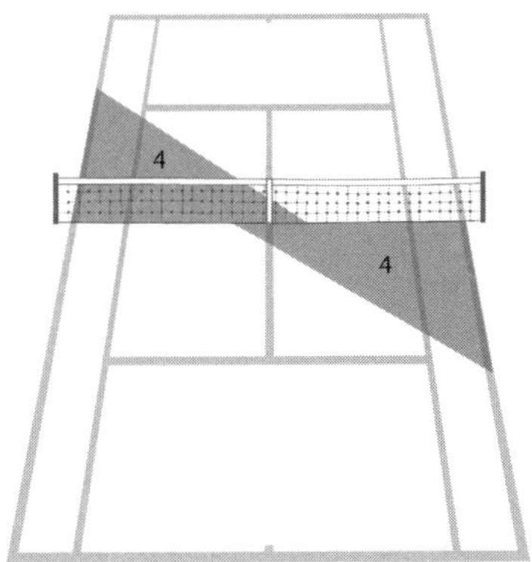

from a Triangle goes into the Diamond and that team puts the ball away for a winner. Where? You're right, Down-the-Middle. What does that tell you? It tells you to NOT hit your shot into the Diamond, if you're in a Triangle.

When you're in the Diamond to hit a ball, you don't have much angle to work with, so your best bet is to hit back down the middle, offensively, depending on the ball and your position on the court. An offensive shot is aimed right at the T with force and power. A defensive lob from the diamond goes deep over the middle and ideally lands on the back center mark by the baseline—where the two triangles meet..

TIP: The decision is yours. Are you in an offensive position from the Diamond? Is the ball above the net? Are you balanced, ready to hit the ball offensively? If so, you should hit at the T in the Diamond. If not, you have to rebuild the point again so you have to find a Triangle. Avoid the terminator.

TRIANGLE TO TRIANGLE.

OFFENSIVE DIAMOND
TO DIAMOND.

DEFENSIVE DIAMOND
TO TRIANGLE.

THE BEAT GOES ON.

NEVER DEFENSIVE TRIANGLE
TO DIAMOND!

I actually draw these triangles on both sides of the net on my teaching court for my students. This way they can see immediately when they hit their shot where they are and where they are aiming.

subtract one.

Let's look at this good ole illustration again. This time note that while there are four Triangles on your opponent's court, only three of them are available to you. They are...the two crosscourt Triangles and the deep one down the line, behind the net player.

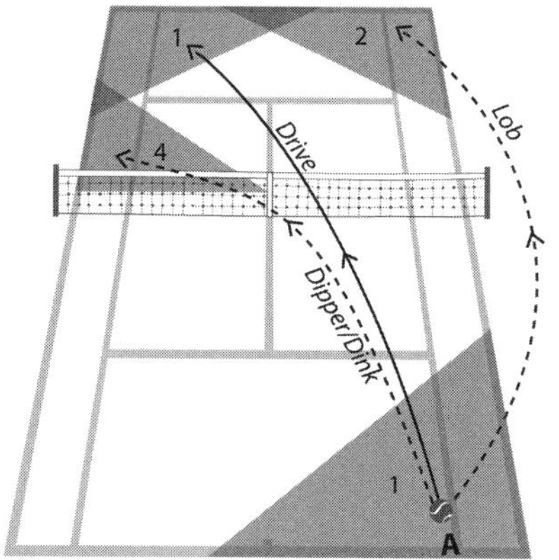

Bet you figured that out before I told you.

Your partner has only three Triangles, too. (Quick, what are

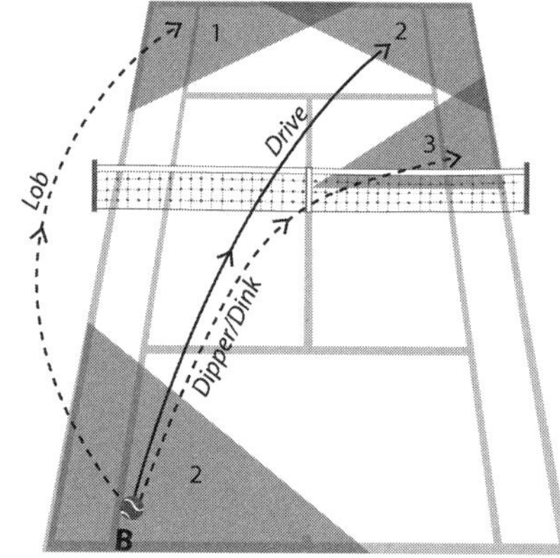

they?) Right, her two crosscourt Triangles and her deep one down the line.

From the deuce court, your choices are 1, 2 and 4. From the add court, your Triangles are 1, 2, and 3. Earlier we talked about your shot selections; here are your targets for those shots.

Okay, let's play some Triangles doubles.

playing the percentages.

If you realize the percentage plays when you see them, you will always be in a point, no matter how horrible a shot you have just hit. (Doesn't that concept make you feel good?) If you obey the Prime Directive and get the ball over the net into your opponent's court, you have kept the ball in play and now *they* must execute and every time someone swings a racquet at a ball, there is a chance of an error. Force them to make the errors and go for low percentage plays, by covering their best percentage shots.

If you're receiving the ball, always try to put yourself in a position to cover the high percentage shot from your opponent. You might not be able to get it back and you may lose the point, but don't give it away, make them earn it. Remember, you may catch them standing there admiring their shot (the way you used to do) and if you just get the ball back over the net, a lot of things can happen.

I'll admit that every once in a while I try for a low-percentage shot and, yes, it usually gets me in trouble, but I never give up on the point. I re-position to cover a high-percentage shot from my opponent. If she decides to play a low-percentage shot, she keeps me in the point. This character flaw of mine also reminds me *why* percentage play is so important and I immediately get back to basics, gnashing my teeth that I broke my own rule by not keeping it simple.

never give up.

Understand this thing about never giving up on a point. The reason most club players give up on a point is because they did not execute a shot the way they had intended. Believe me, if I had given up on a point every time I didn't hit it where I intended I would have taken up bowling by now. You can remove that negative feeling and get your self into the best position to try and recover and make up for your poor execution of the previous shot—just by moving-recovering. Your opponent will feel the pressure and there's a good chance she'll over-hit and press too much. You are *always* in the point until it's over.

Optimists and others call this turning a Negative into a Positive, but it's more than that. It's more because if you can get positioned to receive that high-percentage shot from your opponent, what you're doing is messing with their minds, getting them to go for a different shot the next time. You lose a point, but you gain some vital mental momentum that keeps you in the game and you have to tell yourself that was not a bad exchange. Not bad at all.

Believing you can get to *any* ball will get you far more than if you believe you can get to only some. Play ball—go get 'em*!* I consider every mis-hit as a challenge to see if I can recover and stay in the point and maybe even win the point.

Also, and listen carefully, if you're in position, ready, anticipating, you may be able to step in aggressively and intercept the passing shot and win the point. That'll please you and your partner and the folks on the other side of the net will be looking at the ground and shaking their heads. *They'll also remember what you did with their shot* and perhaps go for their second or third option, lower percentage shots next time.

What you do *now* is part of the whole picture. You may not win this point, but the payoff may come later in the match on a far more important point and that may be just what you need to turn a match around in your favor.

It may (or may not) be a difficult concept to master, but you should know that most matches are won by opponents' mistakes and their inconsistency. Think about it, when you think you're in trouble, your opponents are usually confident and aggressive. This results in drives, passing shots, crisp volleys, power shots mostly down the line and down the middle. Their first choice is not a controlled lob, dropshot, dink, or angled shot.

Conclusion from all this: You and your partner cover the drives, passing shots and crisp volleys. The diagonal workhorse covers the down-the-middle/center crosscourt shot and the terminator covers the down-the-line shot directly at her shot by just blocking the shot and letting the power from an opponent's passing shot carry into her reflex volley. (If you have to explain this to your husband or b.f., remind him that most home runs are hit off fast balls because the pitcher is supplying a lot of the power when the ball connects with the bat.)

the middle ground.

The workhorse always covers the center down the middle passing shots. The terminator covers the passing shot down the line (alley), and her position, hip to T, will make the opponent believe the middle is not open, so she'll go either for the alley or aim more crosscourt, which will now be an easier shot for the workhorse—*and* what we are expecting. If the passing shot is hit at an angle with some power, there's a pretty good chance it will go out. If the lob comes, the danger is over anyway and the pace is slowed. If the workhorse can get to it, you will have survived the passing shot and be right back in the point.

With the lob, you have a chance of hitting an overhead if the lob is the slightest bit too short. Also, the lob has a great chance of going out since most players practice lobs from behind the baseline or from a more defensive position. Remember, if your opponents lob when they could be putting the ball away down at your T(hroat), that should be a signal that a subtle change is taking place in their game and you ought to be aware of such things when you are on the court. It also tells you that maybe they're not as sure about the situation as it first appeared. Stay alert. Never give up.

more shot selection.

One or both of your opponents are in defense which means you and your partner must get to the offense zone and put the pressure on them immediately. Play No Bounce, if you can.

The goal is for you and your partner to get a shot that allows you to get into the attack zone and angle the ball away. That, or make your opponents stay in defense and eventually make a mistake. You must be patient and realize what a tremendous advantage your team has. You will win the point if you can remain patient and play steady and select shots wisely. Stay away from the middle in the beginning and move the opponents from side to side in defense so eventually you will have an opening for the winner down the middle.

If one of your opponents is in offense, *don't* try to hit through her, but rather hit back deep *toward the deepest player*. One of the most important keys to remember in doubles is always hit to the deepest player while building up the point. You must keep your roles and responsibilities and work your overheads so you can take all the lobs that come from defense. You don't have to kill them, but instead concentrate on placing them and make sure you take the lobs in the air so you do not give up your offense advantage.

When you find an opponent who stays back most of the time, you've discovered someone who does not like to volley very much, so what do you do then?

Easy. You try to bring that defense player up to her offense zone with a short soft/low shot to the short crosscourt triangle, and then be ready to hit the volley right back behind her. Mess with her confidence.

A lot of times a player will stay back in the defense zone after a second serve and instead of blasting the return right back at her, you may want to try to hit a short, soft, low return and bring her to her offense zone. NOW YOU'RE REALLY IN CHARGE! She is going to hit up to you and your partner.

You can either lob back over the server or hit a volley back at the area she just left and you have brought the server out of her comfort zone.

Mix it up, but don't be tempted to hit at her partner because she's charged up and ever-ready for volleys. Take advantage, instead, of the fact that whenever you have a player in the defense zone, you can isolate her and play totally against her—Two Against One—from your offense zone and bide your time for a shot to bisect the plane between your opponents and put the ball away. By the way, don't get too close to the net because you'll see some lobs.

Patience.

A note of warning and you see this fairly often on teams you face across the net. If the player in the defense zone is a far-stronger player, you will want to move the ball around with lobs over the net player, short angles and also some hard drives right at the weaker net player, and/or down the middle T.

HELLE'S HINTS

Along with anticipation, remember the three targets that get you out of trouble. Two targets, the #1 and #2 triangles are reached with either drives or lobs. The third target, the #3 or #4, triangle is reached by a low, soft slice dink, or a rolling topspin dipper crosscourt.

20

LESSON TWENTY

shot selection & targets

f-r-o-m triangle #1.

The easiest Triangle to reach and aim for is your opponent's #1 Triangle. Players will recognize #1 to #1 as the very basic doubles drill. You can drive the ball or lob the ball when you aim at this target.

Here's something I want you to *add* to that. Few players are used to actually pointing to exactly where their ball bounces. Oh, they know if it's close to being In or Out, but other than that, they don't make themselves aware of *precisely* where the ball bounces. It's very important to know, because that knowledge tells you what you opponent can do with the ball.

This is defense to defense drill. At times, players hitting the ball will be quite far behind the baseline and recover to their defense home split-step mark after each hit. On the court, hitting from your Triangle #1 to opponents' Triangle #1 should result in a sound like this: "Yes! Yes! Yes!" Practice ten Yes's in a row. Now you know how to hit that target consistently.

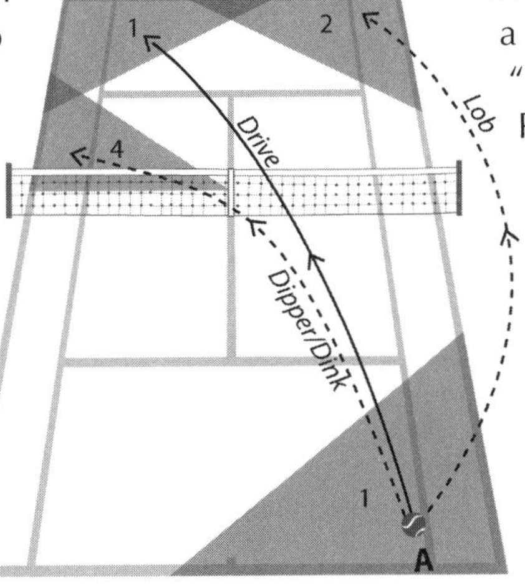

TIP: Depth is important if you're aiming here because if you hit short, your ball will land in the Diamond and your opponents will take over the game.

Your second choice is the short crosscourt Triangle, #4. It's a bit more difficult than the first, but it is still crosscourt and you are not changing the direction of the ball, just hitting it shorter and wider (to avoid the net person). This is an especially good target against a serve-and-volleyer since your shot will be low and into her feet. In the case of a non serve-and-volleyer, you are springing a little surprise and bringing the server to the net unexpectedly.

TIP: Practice taking the ball on the rise while aiming for this triangle.

Take some pace off the ball by slicing it with back spin in order to aim short and low enough and get the angle. A little too deep and you hit the Diamond area and, a little too straight and the net person is having your partner for lunch. A little hard and it goes wide. Practice, practice, practice. The closer you are to the transition zone and the offense zone, the easier this triangle becomes. In order to create this angle from a backhand in the deuce court and the forehand in the ad court, you really need to turn your whole body and hit the ball a little later. It is an "inside out" shot.

Last choice to hit from Triangle #1 is Triangle #2, the deep one down the line in your opponents' defense zone. Your best and safest shot here is a lob because there is usually a net player (terminator) standing in the way of a drive. You can try to make Triangle #2 with a drive, but if your opponent has any brains at all, she'll cut if off before it gets there.

TIP: *Once-in-a-while*, you may want to drive a ball right at the net person to keep her from poaching your crosscourt return. It's always a chancy play and I always consult my partner before I do it to see if she thinks it's a good idea and so she can be ready for it.

If we chose the line drive, my goal is to change direction of the ball and to keep my opponent honest. *It is not to hit a winner.* When I do this, I understand I may lose the point, but that change of direction outweighs the importance of winning that particular point. I don't go down the line experimentally on a game point, but rather at 0-0, ahead 15-0, 15-15, ahead 30-15. Any later in a game, I better be darn sure this change-of-direction line drive is more important than winning the point.

If my partner has just hit down the line, successfully or unsuccessfully, I usually avoid a repeat of that shot because it can backfire on us by waking our opponents up. Using this "wake-up call" too often can charge them up, and help them pick up their game. We don't need that.

I have a Real World story that shows how effective triangles and diamonds can be. During a team competition in one of my last tournaments I was urged again and again by the team captain to hit down the line and practice that chancy shot. I won all my matches, and the championship, and I never had to go for that low percentage down the line shot. I used the three triangles and the diamond. There are plenty of other good targets to explore before I have to resort to the low percentage, selfish, impatient and stupid down the line shot. I have some other words for that shot, but I hope this explains my feelings clearly enough.

In playing the three triangles, you are playing "keep away" from the net player. This way you are tempting your opponents' workhorse to put the ball away and do all the work. You'll discover that most of the time she won't be that patient—so keep doing it. I have three options which are all the responsibility of one player—your opponents' workhorse. You also will tempt their terminator to take certain shots, thereby losing her position and her part of the 100% court coverage. Most players are only ready to defend one or two targets and here I have three! I'm in charge and really working the workhorse. I create confusion on the opposite side of the net. Most teams defend two targets each, but in Dynamite Doubles, the responsibilities are divided 3:1, that is, our workhorse takes three, terminator, one. This is the key to Dynamite Doubles—strategy, not strength.

simple rules.

I know this triangles/numbers game can be a little confusing. On the court, it's easy to show you; on paper, it's a little more difficult, but try this:

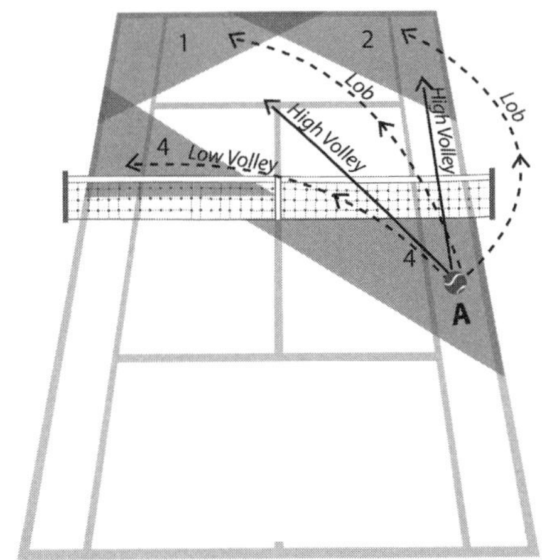

In offense, when you are the workhorse, hitting a high volley, aim down the middle T. When you are hitting a low volley, find a triangle.

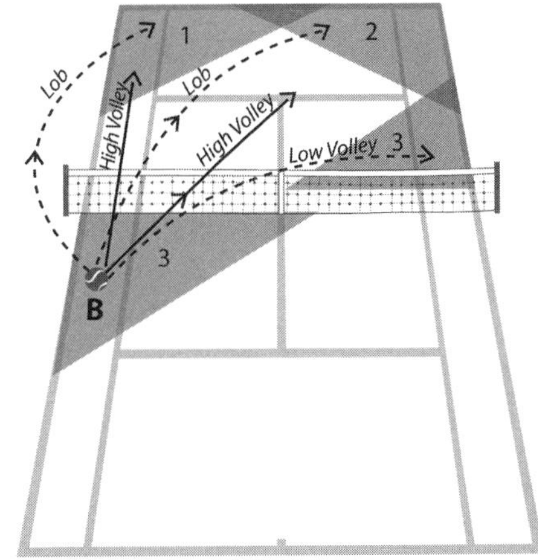

A high volley from the attack zone, you know what to do, Terminate! Hit to the terminator's feet, straight towards a player or angle it out of here!!! BISECT THE PLANE—or bisect the plane between your opponents. A low volley from the attack zone? Find an open triangle and get back into your home in offense.

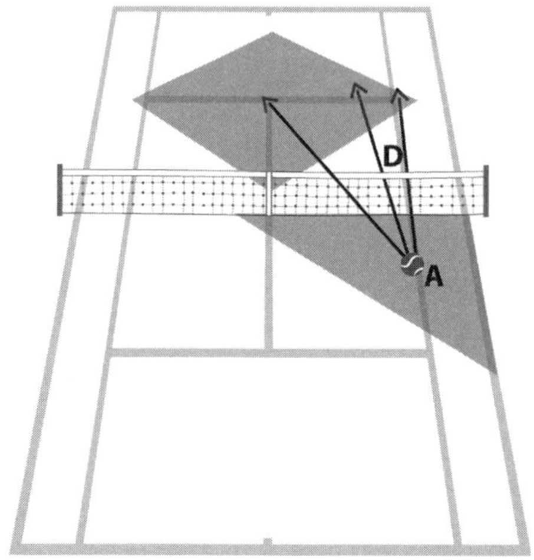

TIP: When your opponents are hitting offensively from their diamond, you should expect a shot back down the diamond on your court and the workhorse is responsible for that shot. In other words, to get as basic as possible, DON'T GET BEAT DOWN THE MIDDLE IF THE BALL IS COMING FROM THE MIDDLE*!*

Get it? Got it. Good.

Bottom line is that you're hitting to the Triangles in order to avoid your opponents' terminator at all cost. *When you are in trouble,* she gets anxious to Terminate and your job is to avoid that. Find one of your three triangles and put your opponents' workhorse to work and in a little while, your opponents will become confused and get their roles mixed up. It's easy to see why: their terminator wants to play, to get into the action, and consequently starts to take shots that are not hers. Conversely, the workhorse also becomes impatient and starts to try to terminate when she should be patient and controlled.

Bingo, your team is playing smart, controlled tennis—and winning.

Here's an easy drill for you and your partner with the ball machine. Put a cone or marker in each of the triangles on the opponents' court and set the ball machine to hit to your #1 Triangle. Now stand in your #1 Triangle "home" and aim at #1 Triangle five times, then #4 five times, with chips or topspin dippers. Then lob to #2 five times.

Got that? Good. Now repeat each shot four times, then three, then two and finally do each one once, and continue rotating between #1, #4 and #2.

Want an extra challenge? Add the line drive down the alley once each rotation is completed—just to stimulate your urgency to hit this selfish, low-percentage shot. In other words, leave this urge on the practice court.

Okay, I realize this is a lot, but if you can arrange to do it, I promise it will do wonders for your game. Remember to practice from both the deuce and ad court. Then practice from your #4 Triangle and practice hitting to triangle #4, #1, and #2. You want to be able to hit any of the three triangles from any one of the triangles on your side any given time. Then you know you can stay in any point and play with the best.

If you constantly rotate and mix up your three triangle targets, your opponents get very confused and then if you hit offensively diamond-to-diamond when the opportunity comes up, you will have used the whole court very efficiently. Remember, you know when to aim for which target, but your opponents don't have a clue.

HELLE'S HINTS

When you are in trouble, find one of your three triangles in order to avoid your opponents' terminator.

When you are NOT in trouble, you don't have to avoid their terminator as much and you can hit more down the middle and at their terminator with power, without having to find a triangle. So you are always either *avoiding* or *going at* your opponents' terminator.

From Triangle #1, my options are:

First Choice: **#1 to #1**
Drive Crosscourt.
Defense to Defense.

Second: **#1 to #4**
Chip or topspin dipper-low over the net. Still crosscourt.

Third: **#1 to #2**
Lob down the line.
Change of direction.

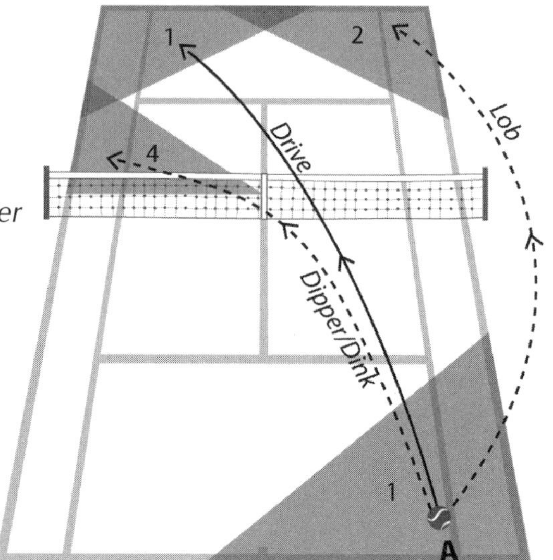

From Triangle #2, my options are the same geometrically, they're just numbered differently:

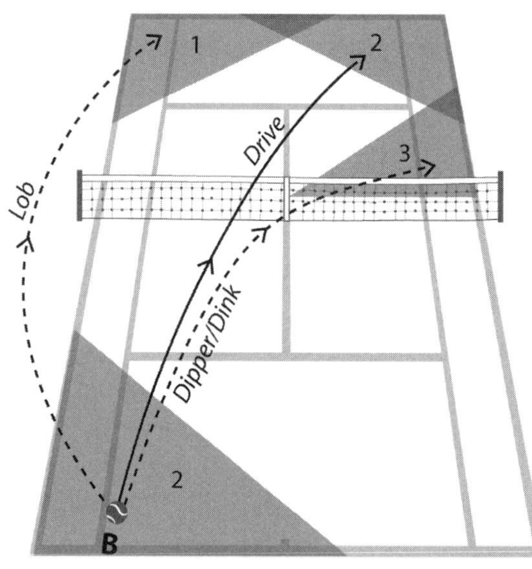

First Choice: **#2 to #2**
Drive Crosscourt.
Defense to Defense.

Second: **#2 to #3**
Chip or topspin dipper—low over the net. Still crosscourt.

Third: **#2 to #1**
Lob down the line.
Change of direction.

21

LESSON TWENTY-ONE

partnerships 101

If you're having a problem with your partner, your game or your opponents, wait until change-over to discuss it. Concentrate on the right and bright things you're both doing and encourage each other. Play your best and give your best effort and it may rub off. Stay in the game and stay with your Plan—until you decide, by mutual agreement, to change it.

At change-over, you can suggest a strategy change—*or listen to a suggestion of one.* Either way, do a fast give-and-take so that you're both on the same page and stick to that plan for the next couple of games. Remember, you play your best tennis when you're relaxed and comfortable with yourself AND your partner. Don't get personal; don't add pressure to her or to yourself because it'll make each of you play at a level less than your potential and before you know it, you'll be out of the match.

And upset and resentful.

And it'll have been another day when something you set out to do for enjoyment has turned into an emotional burden that casts a cloud over your day/weekend/week/month/year. Players always seem to remember the exact number of mistakes their partner made and somehow can't quite remember their own. (Ask your significant other how this works in golf.)

There's one zone I haven't talked about yet and that's the comfort zone. As with the other zones I've been teaching you, *both of you must be in the comfort zone at the same time.* It's going to take two of you to win at this game and there are no winners on the side of the net where lack of confidence, insecurity or intimidation is at play. Your attitude affects you partner's play, so BOTH OF YOU must focus on your common tasks: the ball, the court, the game, your opponents, and not on some real or imagined fault of your partner. Play the hand you're dealt.

If your partner is not doing what you want her to do, tough luck. Adjust your attitude, give her a break. Remember how difficult it is for anyone to change anything about you. It will be impossible to make your partner do anything she doesn't really want to do, or is not capable of doing. You have to adjust, change yourself, accept your partner. And *remember* ... maybe one or both of you is having a bad day. It's up to you to decide whether or not you want to start a fresh, new day right away because you can start anytime. You especially don't want to throw in the towel yet. Anything can happen in tennis and it is NEVER too late to turn a match around. Hang in there with a positive attitude. All you're looking for is to get a foot in the door, to let a little sunshine in. If you help each other get through tough times, by staying positive and focused and by buckling down on the court, then you have grown as a team and you have won. You may lose the match, but you're still a team and there's still tomorrow and tomorrow will be a brighter, better day—for both of you.

Remember the match between Sabatini and Fernandez at the '93 French Open? Mary Joe was down 6–1 and 5–1 in 58 minutes. *Two and a half hours later, she was still out there and winning — 10–8 in the third set!*

Doubles partnerships are like any other partnership, they are not 50/50 as you've been lead to believe. They're made up of two people giving 100/100 to the team. The good ones are made up of very sturdy stuff—respect and understanding, courage and caring, give and take. Good teams, good partnerships begin on the practice court, taking turns to endlessly feed your partner with exactly the shot she wishes to practice, waiting your turn until she does the same for you.

Part of your "mental game" includes retaining the sure and quiet knowledge that together you can win the point, the game, the match. That you are committed to each other and to your team and it's imperturbable continuation. And since neither of you is psychic, that faith and trust comes out in words such as, "That's okay, let's get the next one*!* Good idea*!* Good try*!* Or the universal, No Problem." When you make it impossible for your partner to fail, you make it possible for you both to win.

Saints, as far as we know, don't play doubles tennis. You *are* individuals and there'll be some trying times, but if you have the basics of your partnership worked out and if you practice on keeping the partnership intact, you'll survive the petty strifes that do take place. As I said before, it's not a perfect world, but you can try to make it as perfect as possible when you lace on your shoes and pick up your racquet. Losing a match won't make you enemies, probably won't even affect the price of turnips, so make your commitment to each other and go out there and have *fun* and *dare* anybody to beat this team!

That way you'll be playing the best tennis possible. Partnerships that last a long time improve—on and off the court. Each of you is going to make mistakes. Deal with them and get on with it. Save your real energy for the game and your opponents.

If you see your opponents yelling at each other, engaging in the silly silent treatment, or exchanging sharp looks, smile, you have the match in the bag.

REMEMBER: Don't take yourself so darn seriously! As a team member, if you can find a way to create a smile on your partner's face when things are not going real well, your chances of getting back into the match sooner increase tremendously. It's only a game and being at ease, relaxed, and smiling does make it easier to play well.

DYNAMITE DOUBLES

PARTNERS' CONTRACT

I, ______________________________, hereafter Party of the First Part, being of sound mind and body and desiring to maintain my tennis partnership with

______________________________, party of the Second Part, do hereby declare I will always effort to do the following to ensure my partnership remains equal and sharing and long lasting:

1. I will play in the same major zone as my partner.
2. I will get my first serve in.
3. I will get my return over the net.
4. I will stay in the point until it is over.
5. I will make my lobs high, knowing height is more important than depth.
6. I will always make my Split-Step just before my opponent hits the ball.
7. I will BISECT THE PLANE of our opponents when I am the terminator.
8. I will hit a minimum of 3 shots with patience when I am the workhorse.
9. I will be positive and focused and in-the-game at all times.
10. I will let go of the last point played. I will not worry about the end result.

I will stay in the moment and play One Point At A Time.

SIGNED THIS ________ DAY OF ______________________ (month), ____________ (year):

____
signature

DYNAMITE DOUBLES

PARTNERS' CONTRACT

I, ________________________________, hereafter Party of the First Part, being of sound mind and body and desiring to maintain my tennis partnership with

________________________________, party of the Second Part, do hereby declare I will always effort to do the following to ensure my partnership remains equal and sharing and long lasting:

1. I will play in the same major zone as my partner.
2. I will get my first serve in.
3. I will get my return over the net.
4. I will stay in the point until it is over.
5. I will make my lobs high, knowing height is more important than depth.
6. I will always make my Split-Step just before my opponent hits the ball.
7. I will BISECT THE PLANE of our opponents when I am the terminator.
8. I will hit a minimum of 3 shots with patience when I am the workhorse.
9. I will be positive and focused and in-the-game at all times.
10. I will let go of the last point played. I will not worry about the end result.

I will stay in the moment and play One Point At A Time.

SIGNED THIS ________ DAY OF ________________________ (month), ____________ (year):

____

signature

questions & answers

These are most frequently-asked questions from my students. We may have covered some of this material in the book, but here are the things most people learning the Dynamite Doubles / Diagonal want to know.

Who takes the down-the-middle shot?
The workhorse—the player diagonally across from the ball.

How do we protect against the lob?
Answer 1: Do not get into the attack zone. Stay in the offense zone and let the workhorse take the majority of the lobs. Practice your overheads. Anticipate.
Answer 2: Go Australian.

My partner (I) have a weak serve.
Answer 1: Take a lesson.
Answer 2: Placement is everything in doubles. Keep your serve deep and vary your placement. Until your serve gets stronger, you may have to stay back in the defense zone after serving in order to get into the point. Your partner can also come back with you if need be. Remember, you can play winning doubles from the defense zone

Our opponents hit so hard we're helpless.
Play as a team from the defense zone to give yourselves time to adjust to their powerful hits. Once your opponents make a few errors and you feel more comfortable, you can then work your way back to the offense zone. Or you may choose to stay back since it is winning for you. By moving back to defense, you have moved the targets of your opponents, remember.

Our opponents seem to hit all evil angles.
Hit your balls straight and down the middle, to decrease the angle on your shot. Lobs straight and over the middle neutralize angles a great deal, too.

We get beat down the alley all the time.
Where is your terminator? That's the only shot the terminator is responsible for. She needs to be ready for it. She must be looking for that shot. If that does not work, stop hitting crosscourt and change to more straight ahead, down-the-middle shots. You can also in this situation both go back to defense and play from there.

Why is it I just can't win?
You're probably focusing on the outcome rather than staying in the moment, Playing One Point At A Time. Focus on what you can do now, rather than what you feel you can't. Also, you may be afraid. Remember, Fear = Future Expectations – Anticipated Results. Have a simple, doable plan for each point and focus on executing that plan.

Our opponents have a reputation for giving bad calls and playing mind games. What do we do?
Stay mentally on your side of the net, communicate with your partner, display a good attitude and play tennis. Ignore them as much as possible. Play tough Dynamite Doubles and play one point at a time. If you get a few bad calls and you are both sure of it, you can ask for a court monitor and usually the presence of a third party eliminates any problems.

Why can't I make it up to the offense zone with my partner, without getting the ball at my feet?
You may be spectating after your shot, instead of moving rapidly. Remember, you should know prior to your hit where you are going afterward. Be physically in the transition zone when hitting the ball and then pro-

ceed to offense. Split-step/hop prior to your opponent's stroke. It is too far to travel from defense to offense in one shot, except for the lob.

My partner doesn't come in. What can I do alone up in offense?
There are two ways to look at this. First, if your partner can control the defense and set up the point for you to Terminate, you can stay up in offense patiently. If that doesn't work, you have to come back to defense with your partner and play winning doubles from there. Give and take, but do whatever it takes to make it work. Being in the same major zone together is more important than anything else.

I play a lot against a woman who's six feet tall and has extremely long arms. She's intimidating to say the least. Suggestions?
Focus on the ball and the open targets. No matter how tall or big a player, there is always an open triangle on the court for you to exploit. OR aim toward her body and feet and let her tangle up those long arms.

Okay, here's a tough one. I hate to play lefties. Does Dynamite Doubles work against them?
Lefties, righties, one-handed, two-handed—Dynamite Doubles—The Diagonal Way... works against ALL of them. It's geometry and court coverage, so whether you play a lefty or a righty, you still move to position yourself in the same spot in relation to your partner and to the ball.

The system plays the ball, the court and the opponents, so not to worry.

Can I ever use all four triangles?
Yes. When your opponents' terminator is not in her offense-terminator position, the fourth triangle is open for you to use.

A minute ago you mentioned playing Australian. How and when should we do that.

I thought you'd never ask! Australian means change. If you are not winning your service game by the conventional positions, Australian may be the solution. Australian is also called the I-Formation, because of the placement of server and partner before the serve. I have 3 ways of playing the Australian formation, which will give you yet more options to change your strategy and win the next point.

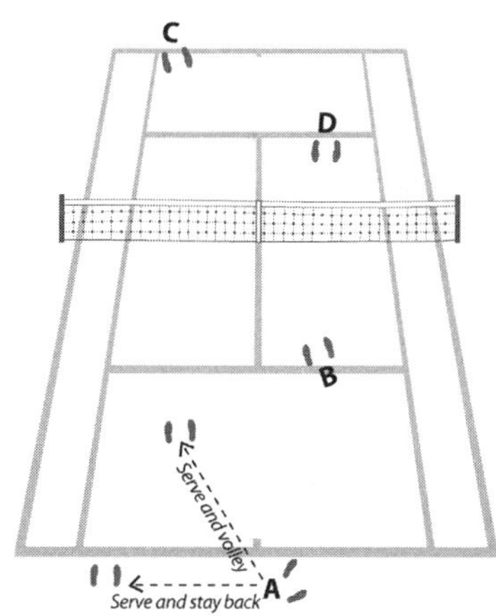

❶ Server A stands close to the center mark while partner B is straight in front of her on the same side of the court on the service line facing the returner. A and B have switched roles. B is no longer the terminator, but the crosscourt workhorse, who takes all lobs, cross courts and middle balls. A is going to be the terminator, and therefore has to move over to cover the down-the-line shot. Whether A is serving and volleying, or serving and staying back, she needs to hit straight back to C, the deepest player, and avoid D, who is anxious to hit the ball toward B's feet. So no crosscourt in the Australian formation. Hit to the deepest player until you get the chance to bisect then plane between the opponents. Yes, Patience is the key once more

❷ Server A stands close to the center mark while partner B is in the top of the offense zone close to the attack zone on the opposite side of A, still close to the center line, and thus able to move to either side once the serve has been hit. B is terminating either way trying to cut off the return and win the point, and not worried about the lob at all. B has to give a signal to server A as to which

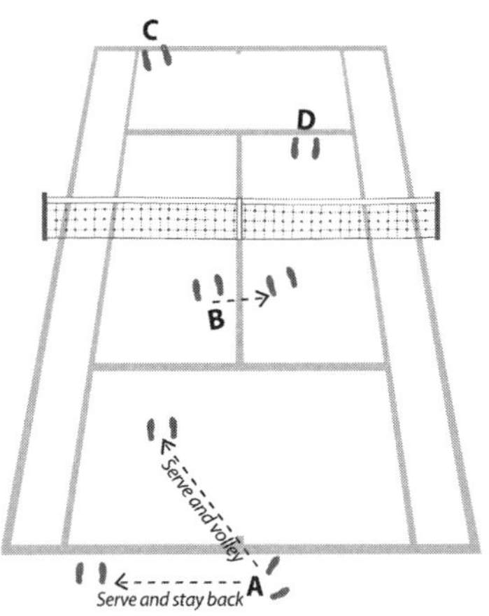

way she is going and A then moves to the opposite side and takes all lobs no matter what.

❸ Server A stands close to the center mark with partner B back in the defense zone with

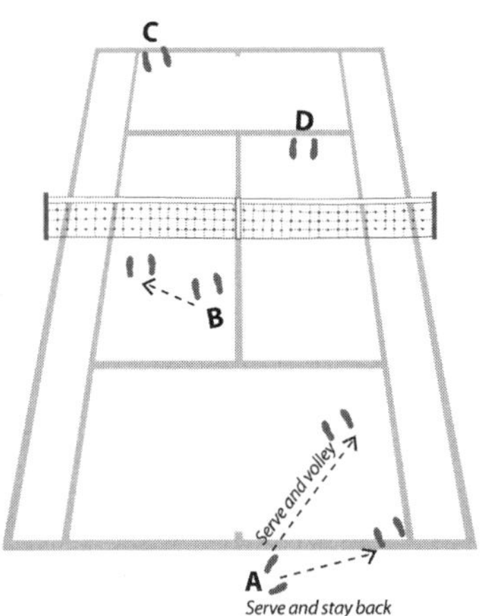

her on the same side of the center mark but out wide waiting for the crosscourt. B has been made the crosscourt workhorse and is facing the returner. In the deuce court B is to the right of the server and in the ad court to the left. Server A moves to the open court after serving.

This last option is the most defensive of them all but is very effective at times. By making the server's partner the workhorse right after the serve is hit takes some pressure off the server, gets the partner more involved in the point and gives the opponents something new to think about.

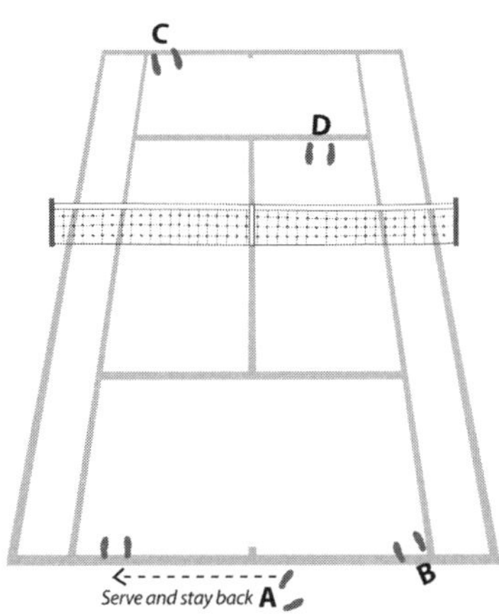

In summary, you use the Australian Formations to change the momentum of the game by giving your opponents a "new look" when they are returning. You're trying to break their concentration, their momentum and tempt them to go for a more difficult and perhaps unfamiliar return. Certainly, you'll be getting in their heads a bit, perhaps enough to turn the game, set and match in your favor.

Here it is, Helle's handy-dandy **seven-pointed star**, the basic rules you can take to the court and play winning doubles—today.

1

Always face where the ball is coming from and let the ball come into your "V".

2

Know your "home" positions on the court—
2 in offense zone, 2 in defense zone, depending on whether you are the workhorse or the terminator.

3

Know your responsibilities as a terminator and as a workhorse.

4

Recover to a major zone AFTER your hit and BEFORE your opponent's hit.

5

READY, READ and REACT*!*
When the ball you hit bounces in your opponents' court, get Ready to split-step as your opponent's racquet moves to strike the ball, so you can Read what is coming and React to the oncoming ball.

6

A point is never over until the ball bounces the second time. Never give up. There are no put-aways! HANG IN THERE. The ball is always coming back*!*

7

Doubles is a game of angles and percentages.
And Patience.

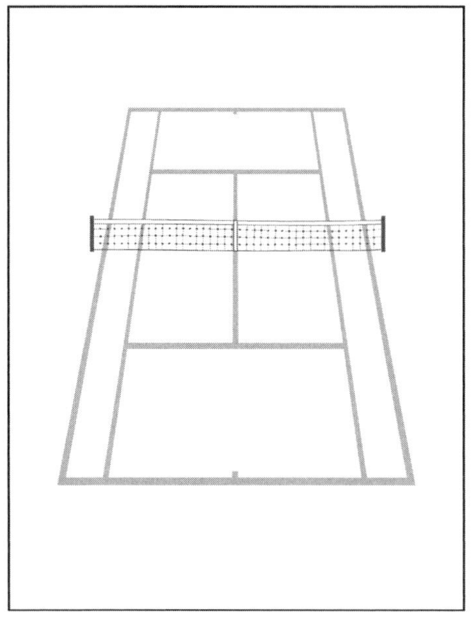

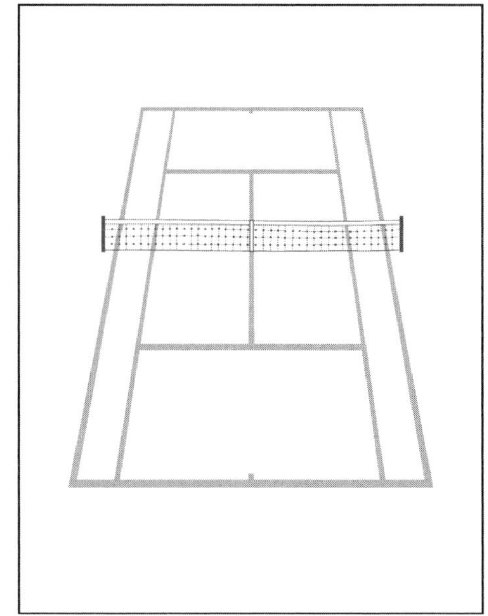

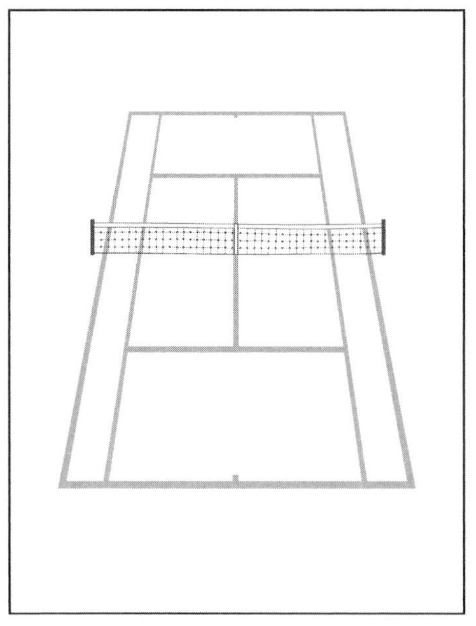

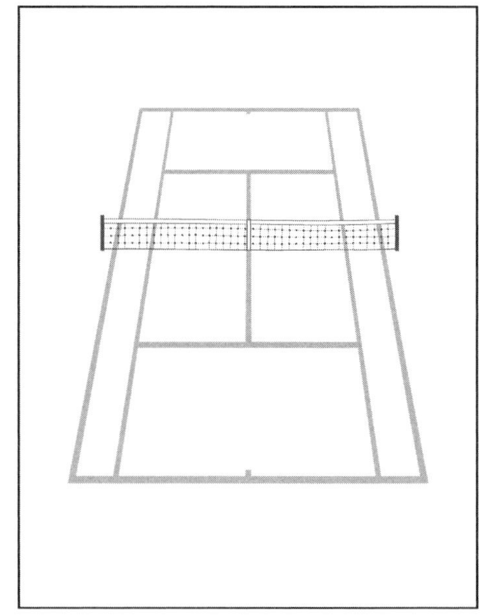

Send to: DYNAMITE DOUBLES, 41 Flicker Drive, Novato, California 94949 USA

ORDER A COPY OF *DYNAMITE DOUBLES* FOR YOUR PARTNER!

Yes! Please send me __________ copies of Helle's book, *Dynamite Doubles.*

☐ I enclose a check or $29.95 (incl. tax + handling) for each copy

NAME

ADDRESS

CITY STATE ZIP

PHONE NUMBER

Please have Helle autograph the book(s) as follows:

You can also order online at www.dynamitedoubles.com

ORDER A COPY OF *DYNAMITE DOUBLES* FOR YOUR PARTNER!

Yes! Please send me __________ copies of Helle's book, *Dynamite Doubles.*

☐ I enclose a check or $29.95 (incl. tax + handling) for each copy

NAME

ADDRESS

CITY STATE ZIP

PHONE NUMBER

Please have Helle autograph the book(s) as follows:

You can also order online at www.dynamitedoubles.com

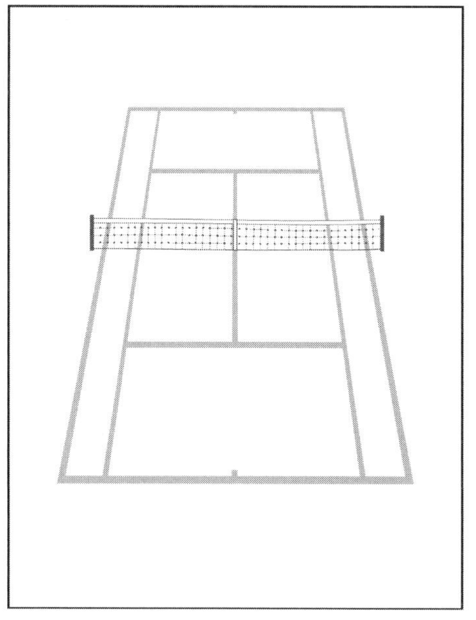
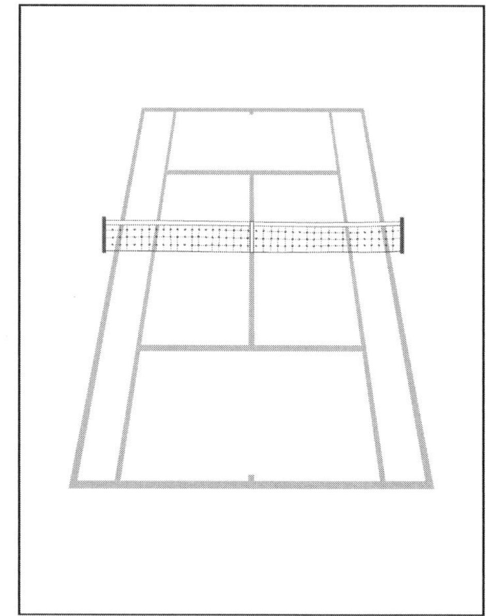
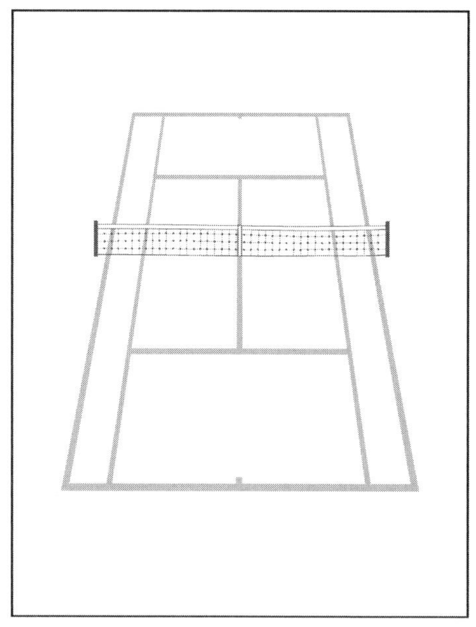
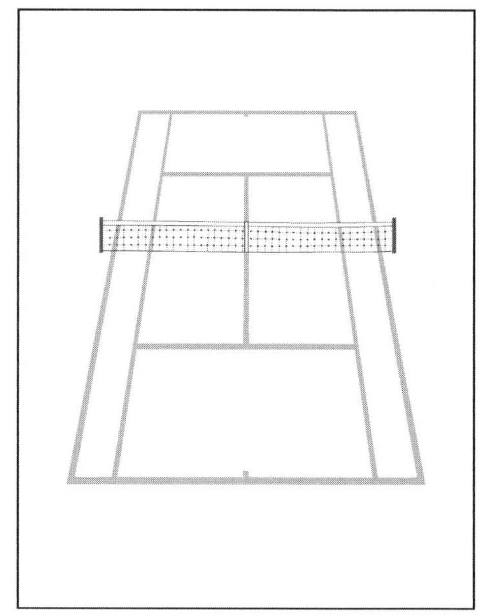

Send to: DYNAMITE DOUBLES, 41 Flicker Drive, Novato, California 94949 USA

ORDER A COPY OF *DYNAMITE DOUBLES* FOR YOUR PARTNER!

Yes! Please send me __________ copies of Helle's book, *Dynamite Doubles*.

☐ I enclose a check or $28.50 (incl. tax + handling) for each copy

NAME

ADDRESS

CITY STATE ZIP

PHONE NUMBER

Please have Helle autograph the book(s) as follows:

ORDER A COPY OF *DYNAMITE DOUBLES* FOR YOUR PARTNER!

Yes! Please send me __________ copies of Helle's book, *Dynamite Doubles*.

☐ I enclose a check or $28.50 (incl. tax + handling) for each copy

NAME

ADDRESS

CITY STATE ZIP

PHONE NUMBER

Please have Helle autograph the book(s) as follows:

You can also order online at www.dynamitedoubles.com

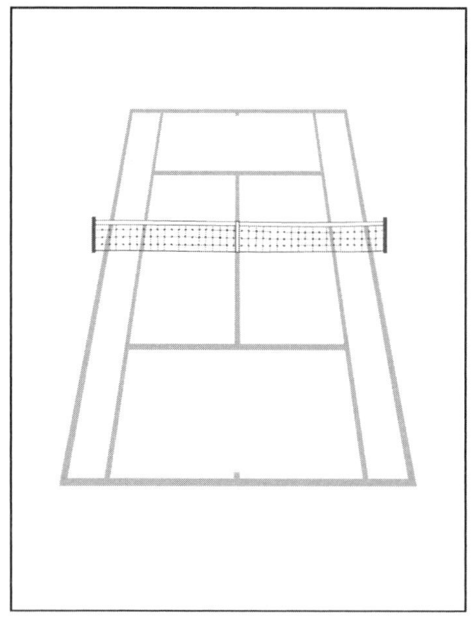

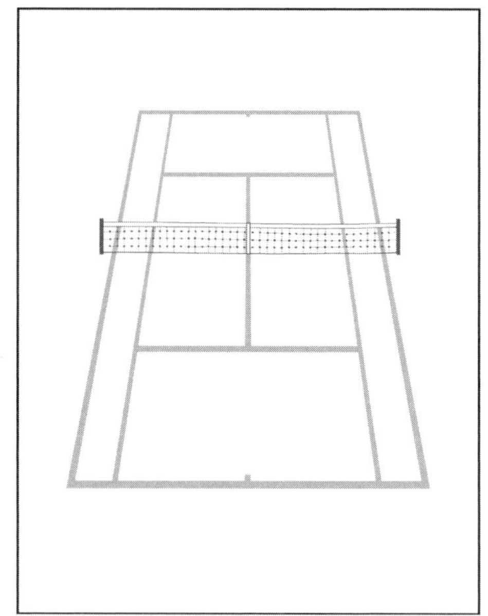

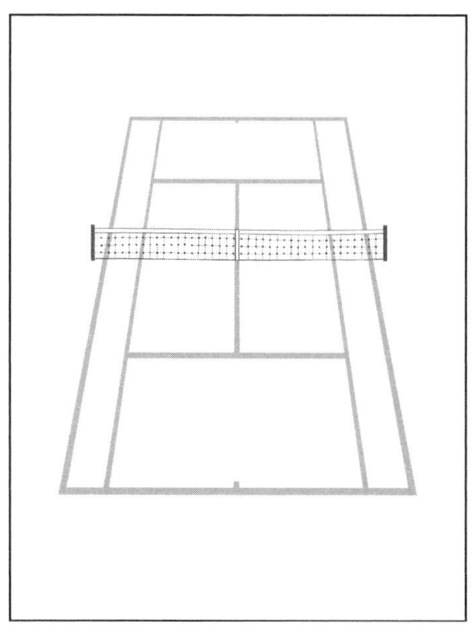

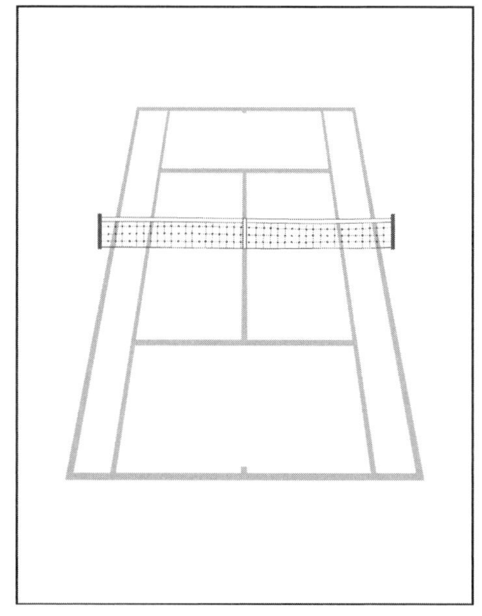

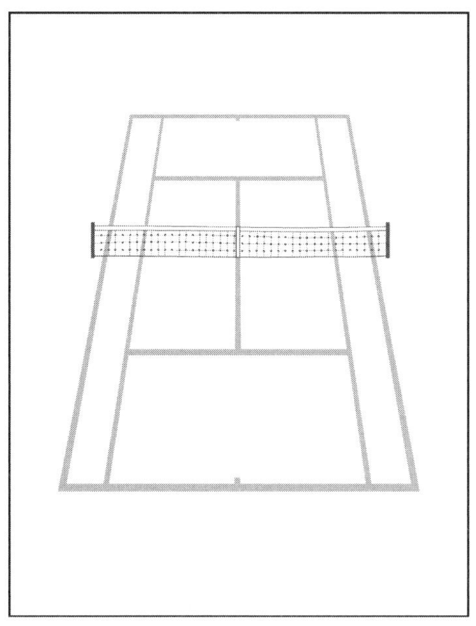

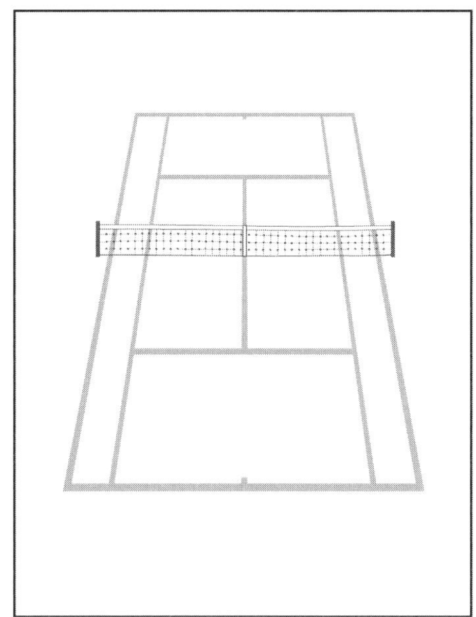

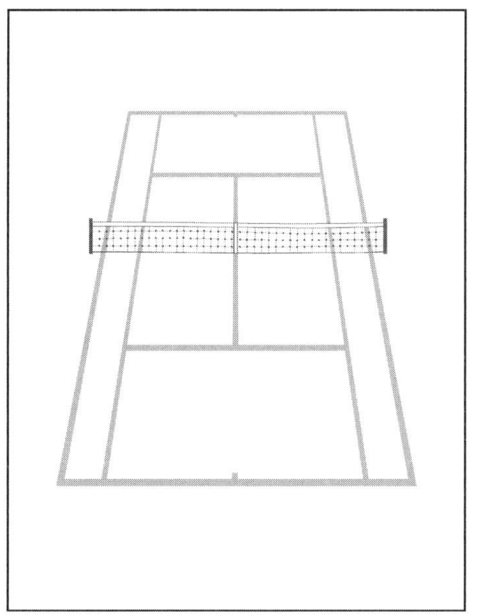

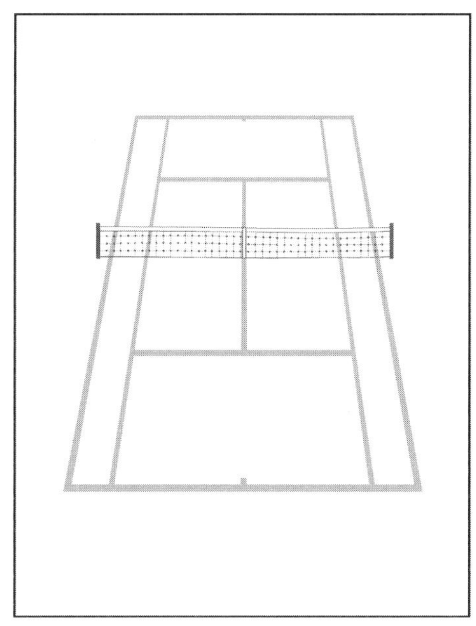

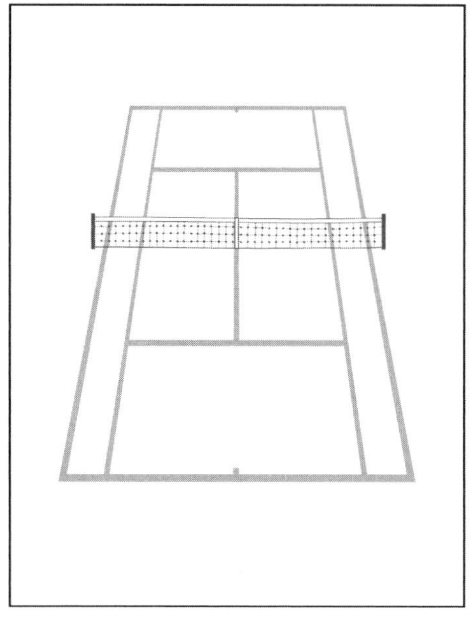

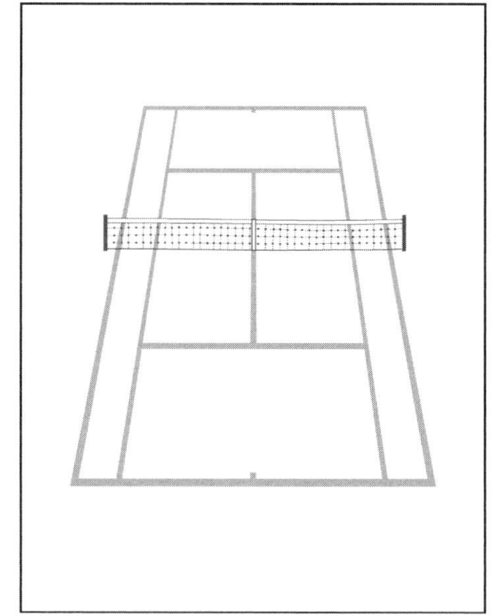

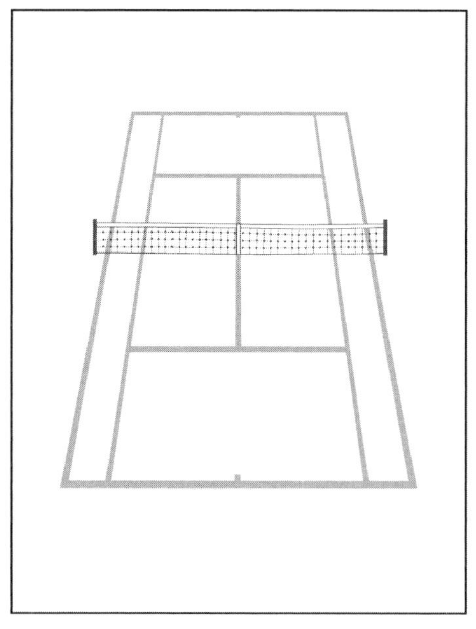

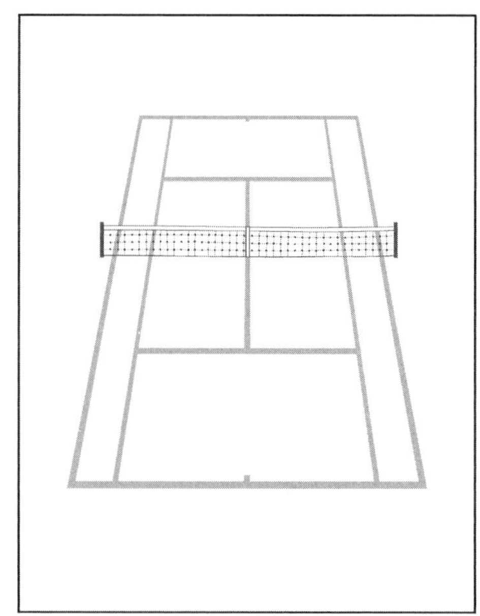

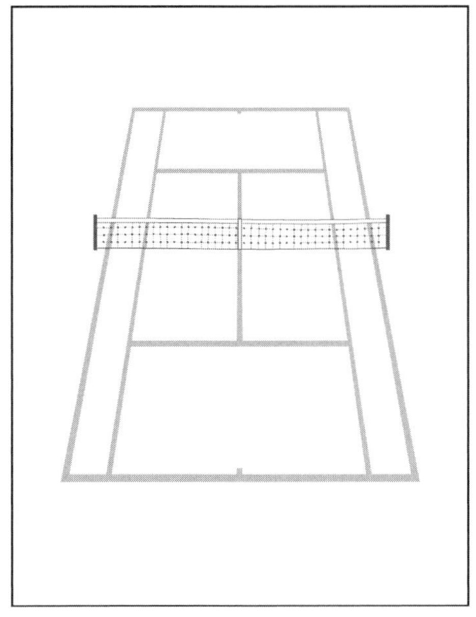

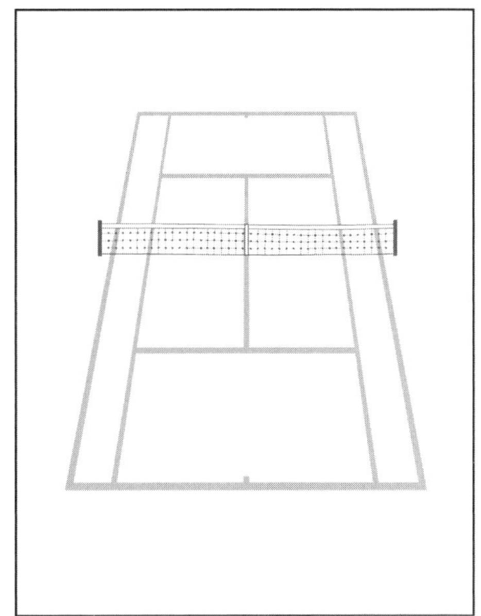

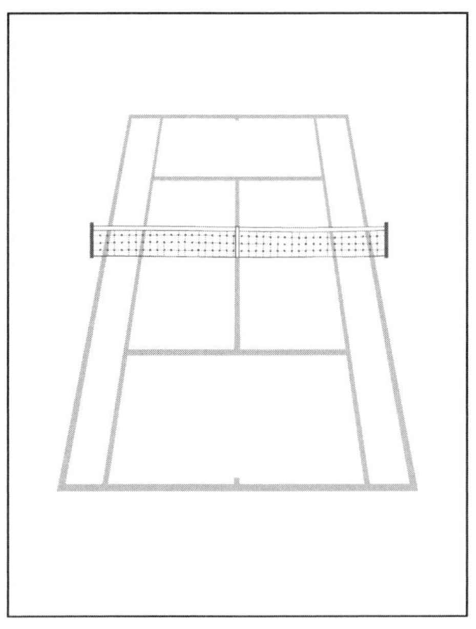

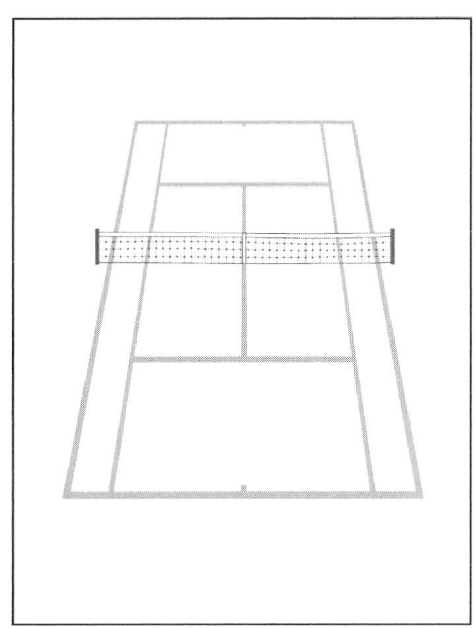

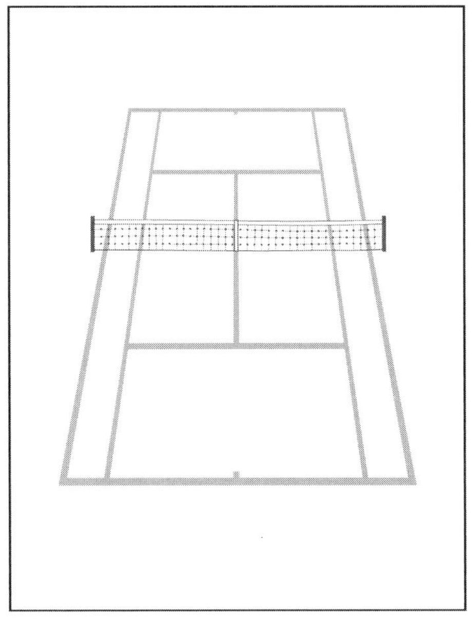

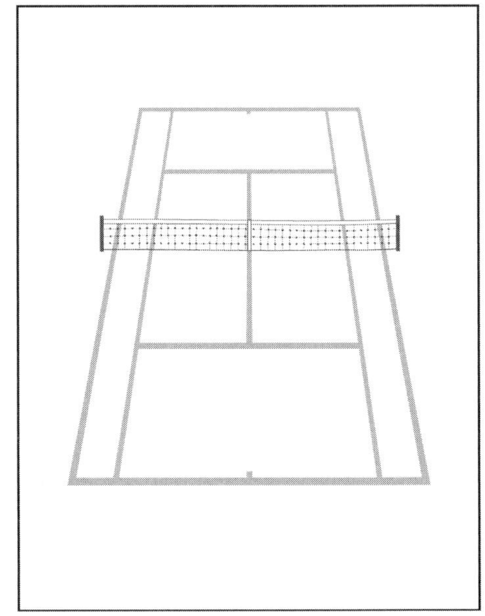

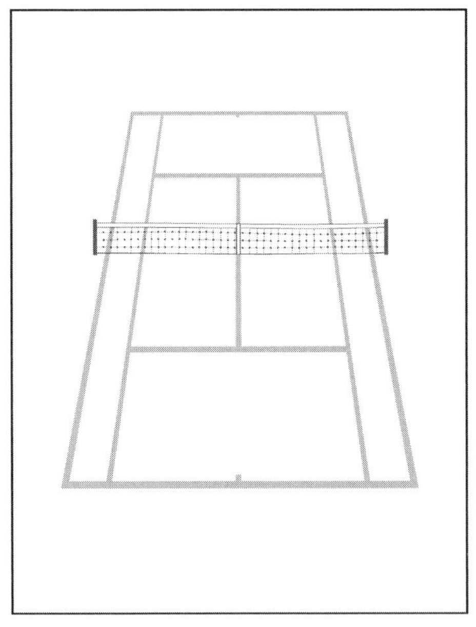

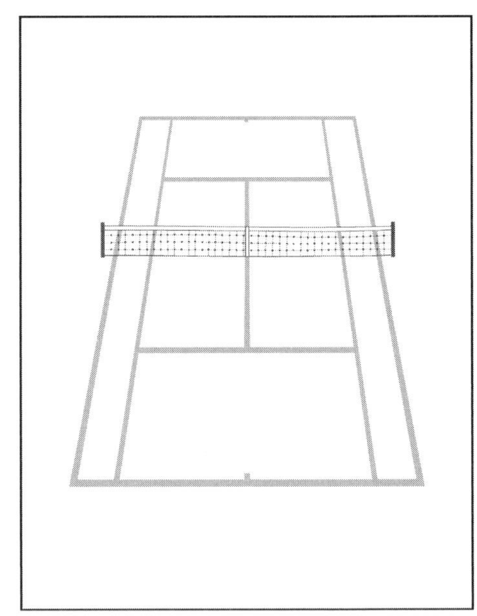

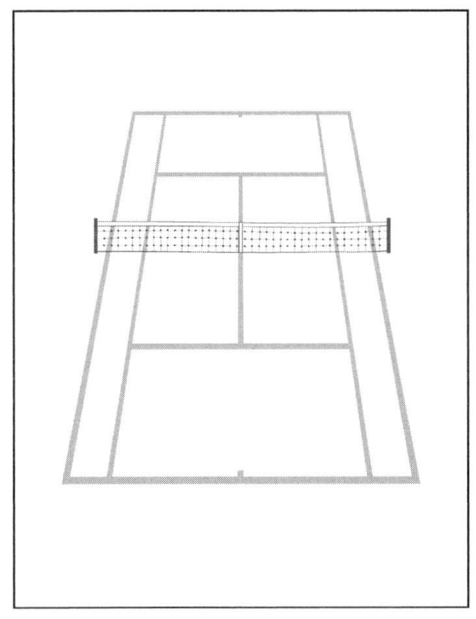

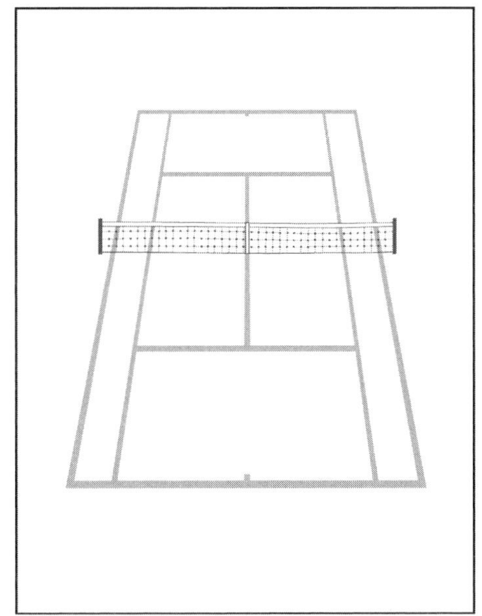

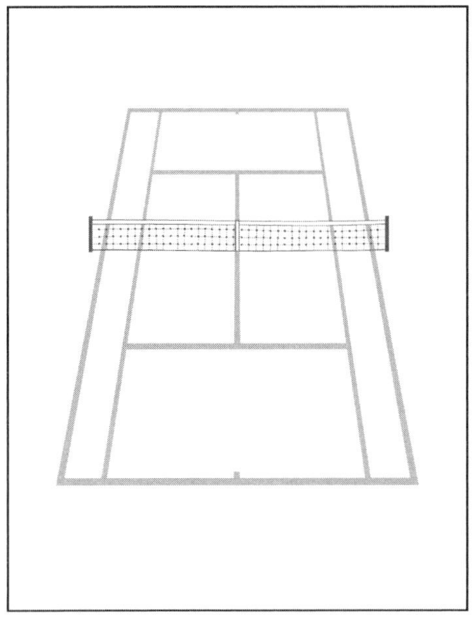

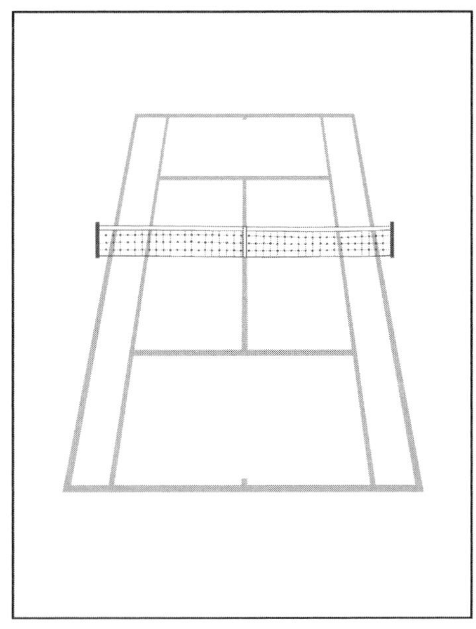

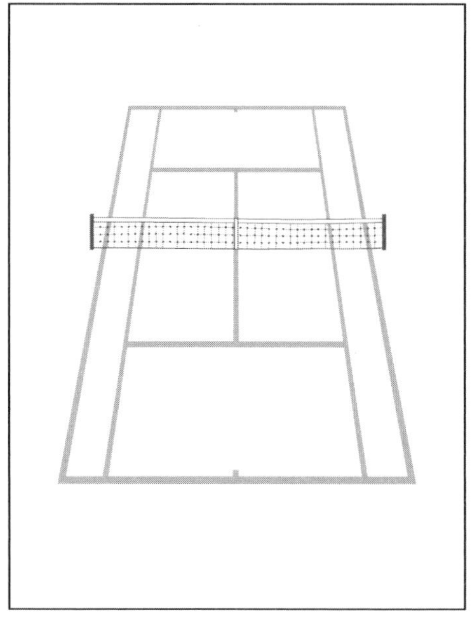

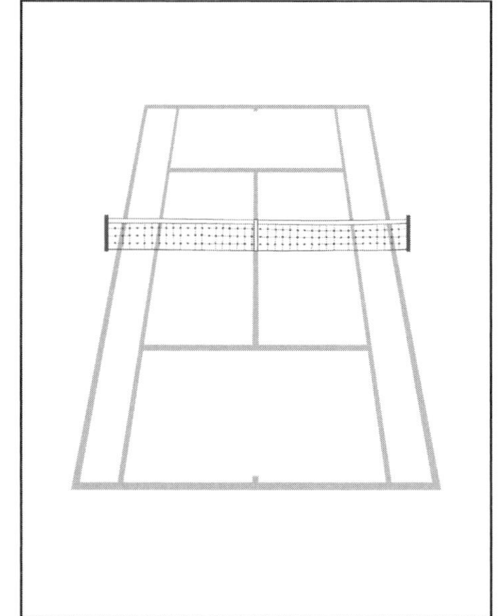

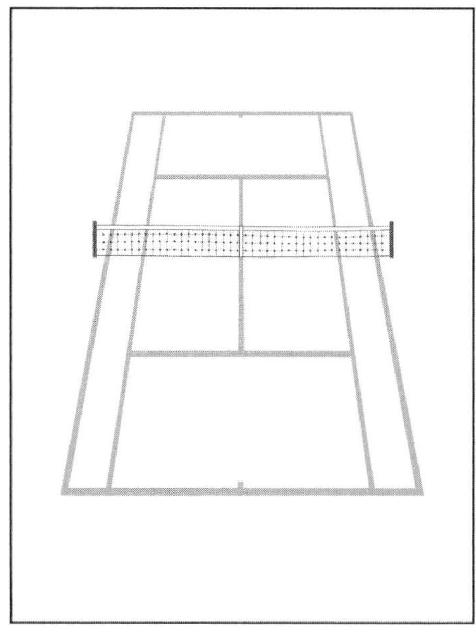

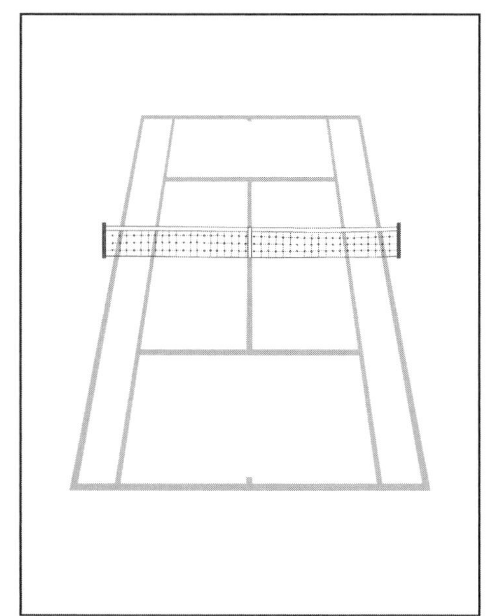

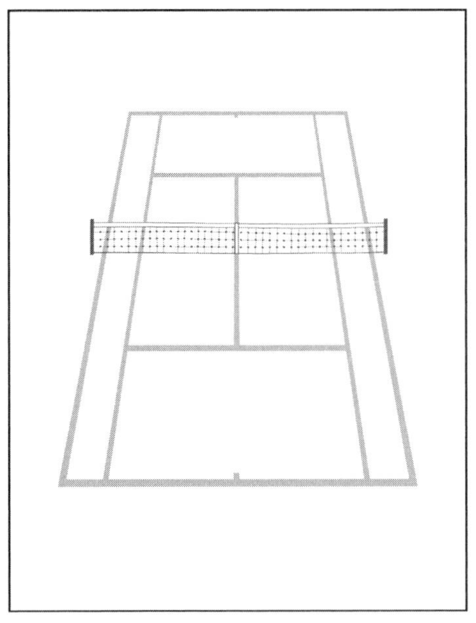

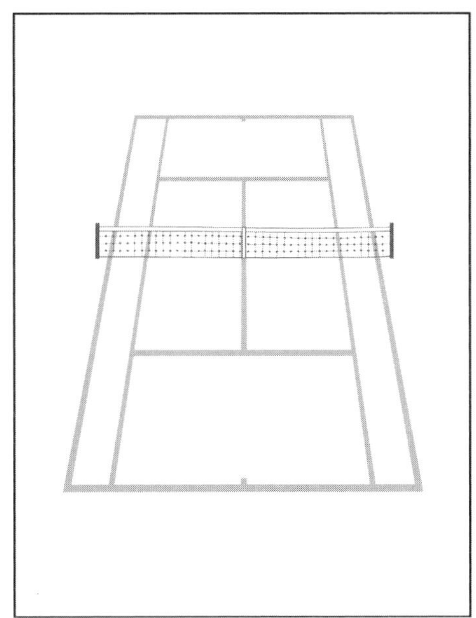

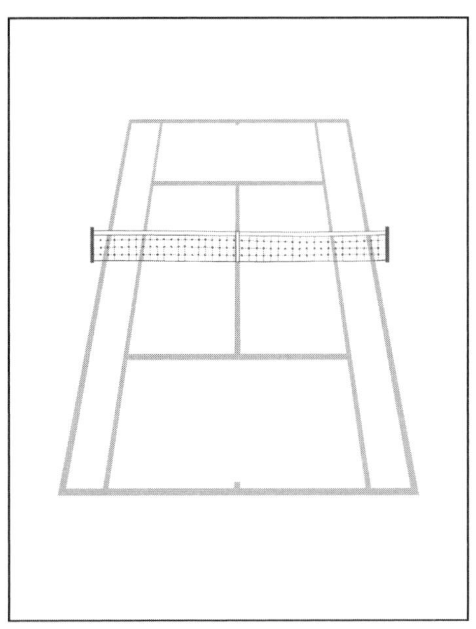

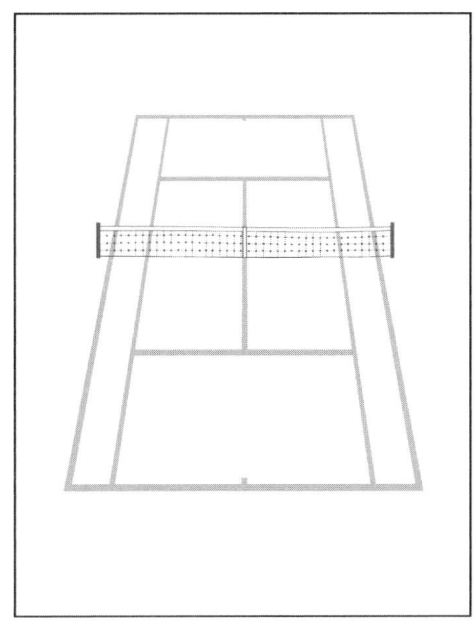

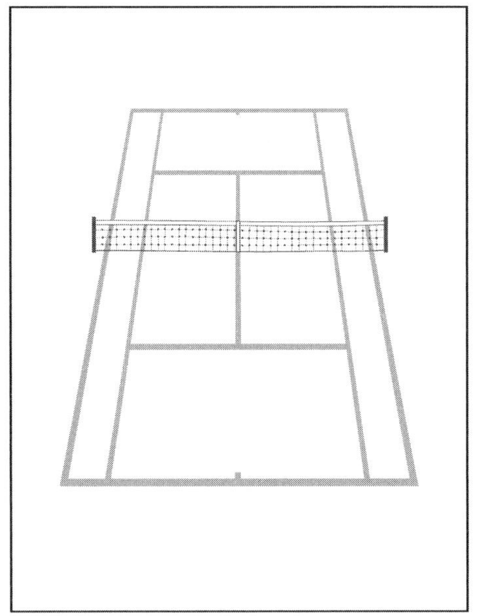

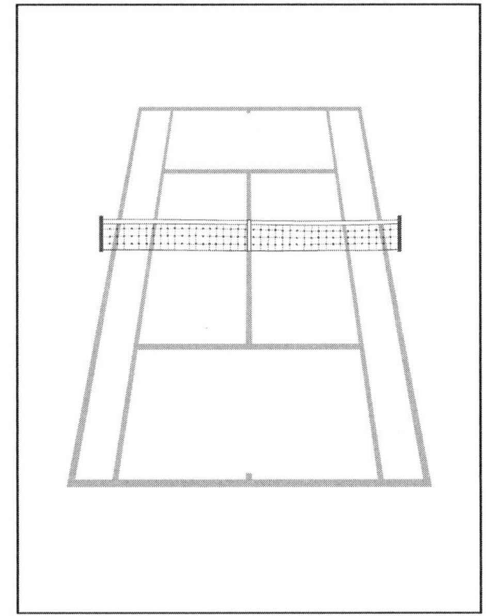

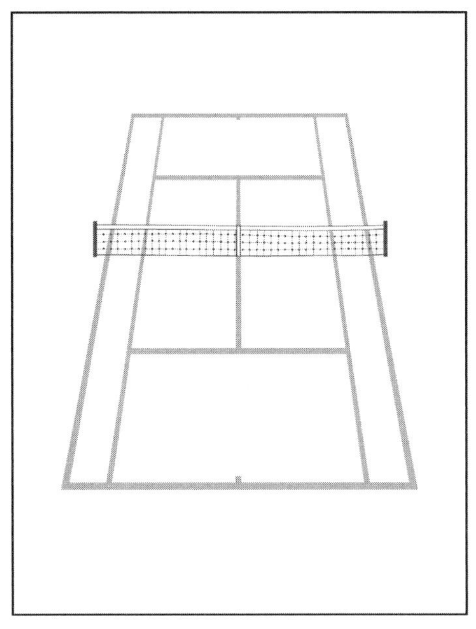

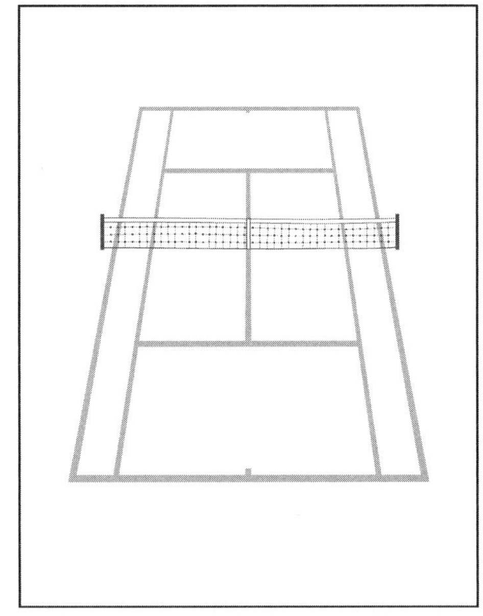

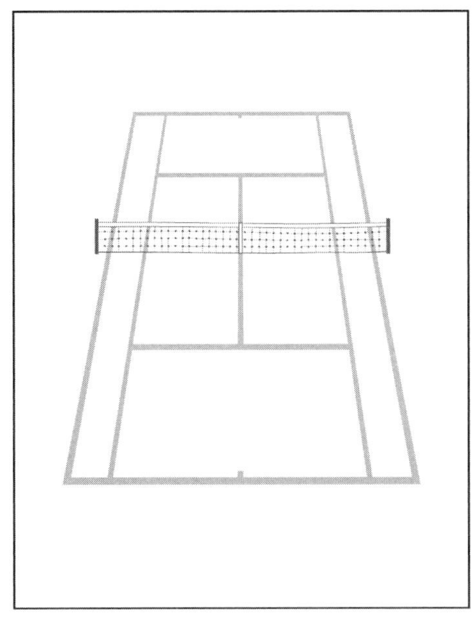

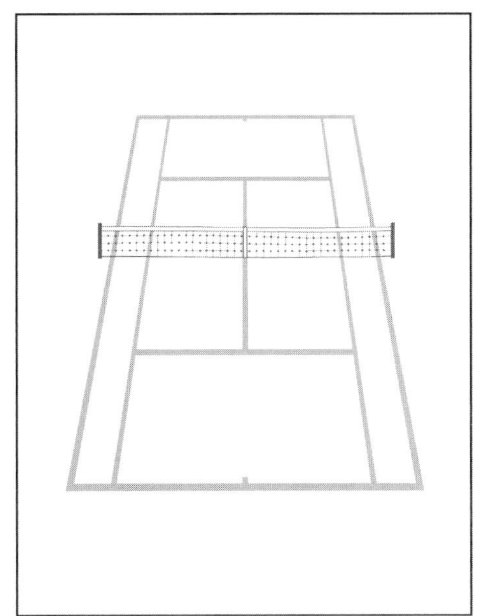

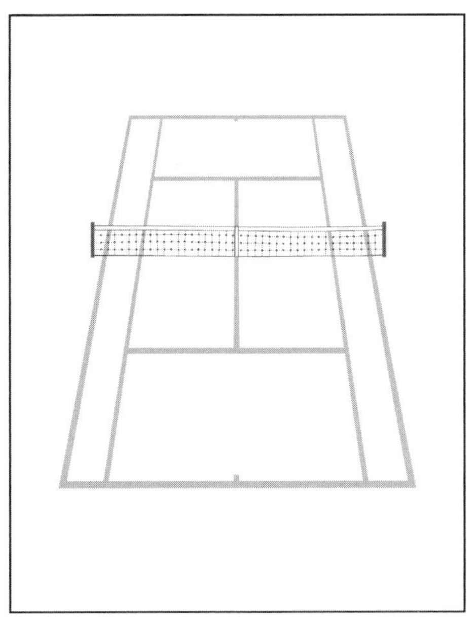

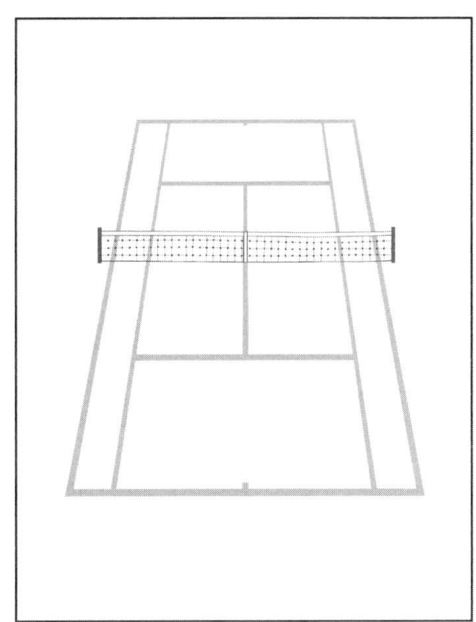

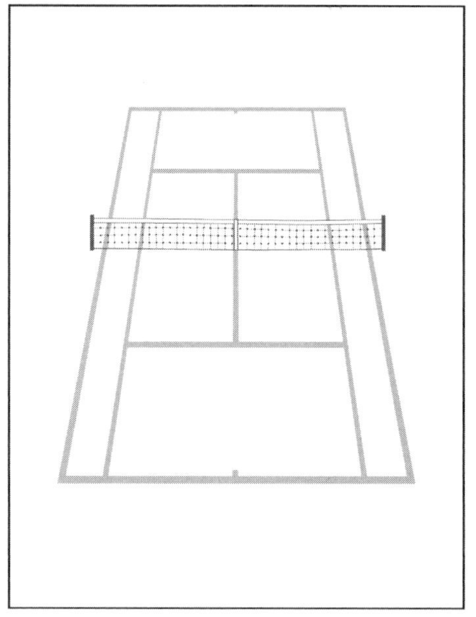

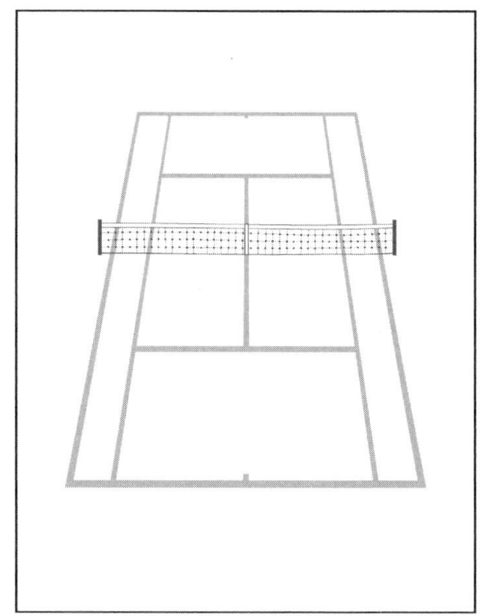

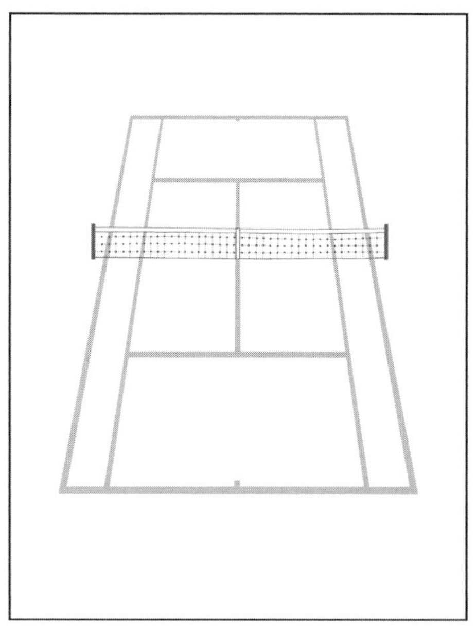

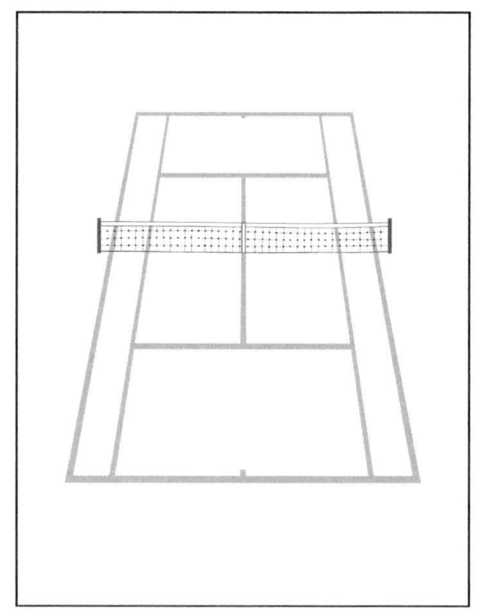